II Deepawali II
pooja-vidhi

(an easy step-by-step pooja-guide)

mythology, rituals & mantras with
shree sukta and aarti of lakshmee ji

Compiled, translated and edited by
Pawan Kumar Mishra

tara
India Research Press
Flat. 6, Khan Market, New Delhi - 110 003
Ph: 24694610; Fax : 24618637
www.indiaresearchpress.com
contact@indiaresearchpress.com

First published in 2005

REVISED AND UPDATED
2020

ISBN 13 : 978-81-8386-183-0

Printed and Bound in India for
Tara Press-India Research Press

This work is dedicated to

Pooja

the path of worship,
that leads to enhanced awareness of
the Divine Romance,
of our souls with the Soul of the Universe...

Contents

Part I

Deepawali - Poojan

(Essence, Rituals and Process)

Deepawali
Deepening of the Light

Of Darkness and Light

Darkness represents all the negative actions and thoughts, arising out of ignorance. The Upanishads frequently use an example to illustrate this. A person sees a snake across his path in the dark, and screams. He is gripped with fear, and sees himself being bitten by the snake, and dying of poison. He begins to sweat, and tremble. His friend hears his scream, and rushes to him with a torch of fire. In the light, the man sees that there is no snake. What he thought to be a snake, is actually a rope! He relaxes. Fear disappears. The rope was not a snake. The snake did not become the rope. Due to darkness, and ignorance, the image of snake that was there in the person's mind, got super imposed on the shape of the rope lying on the ground. Almost how image imposition is carried out to morph the faces of celebrities, by using the photo-shop software! The moment darkness is removed by light, it causes ignorance to disappear, and understanding to dawn. True perspective is gained. A rope is seen as a rope, not as a snake.

Hence, light is celebrated universally. In fact, darkness has no existence. Darkness is only the absence of light. Not all the darkness of the world can put off the light of a single small candle. It is better therefore, to light a candle and celebrate enlightenment, than to curse the darkness, and remain caged in it. Enlightened mind is not just like a bird flying free, but such a mind *becomes* the sky itself!

tamso maa jyotir gamaya, seeks the Upanishad, meaning, "from darkness, lead me unto light".

Shree Vidya Maa Mahalakshmi- The Presiding Deity

Shree Vidya is understood to be the Universal Mother or the Primordial Feminine Energy also called *Shakti* in sanskrit. She is referred to as the Devi (the Goddess), Tripura Sundari (the Beauty of the Three Worlds), Shodashi (the Sixteen), Mahaa Lakshmee or simply, Maa (the Mother). She is beyond comprehension of human mind, especially the conscious mind, which is but a tiny fraction of the total mind. She cannot therefore be "known" by common logical thinking and rationalisation. She can be "experienced" as an awareness of deep joy and love, of indescribable positive energy in moments of deep silence. She is the substratum of all creation and beyond. She permeates and transcends at the same time, all that is known, and that is not.

To simplify, She is the stir of Energy in the Pure Potential, called Shiva. Without Her, Pure Potential Shiva would never be differentiated sufficiently to manifest into this universe. She makes creation possible. She is the Creatrix. No words describe her better than the following from the Isha Upnishad, an ancient Vedic text. It refers to a state of awareness when a glimpse of Goddess is obtained as Pure Energy.

It is not outer awareness,

It is not inner awareness,

Nor is it a suspension of awareness.

It is not knowing,

It is not unknowing,

Nor is it knowingness itself.

It can neither be seen nor understood,

It cannot be given boundaries.

It is ineffable and beyond thought.

It is undefinable

It is known only through becoming it.

Sages visualised Her as being seated on a lotus emanating from the navel of Shiva. Shiva Himself lying down on a couch, of which the four legs are Brahma (the Creator), Vishnu (the Sustainer), Shankara (the Destroyer), and Ishwara (the Owner) of this Universe. She has four hands which hold a lotus, a bow made of sugarcane, flower tipped arrows, and a goad. This imagery of the Goddess has an extremely deep meaning, which cannot be explained within the scope of this work.

So entwined is the worship of Shree Vidya in India amongst Hindus, that every Hindu male has Shree prefixed to his name. Married females have Shreemati, and unmarried females have Sushree prefixed to their names. The English word "Sir" is derived from "Shree". "Sir" denotes a person knighted by the British Queen, and is supposed to be well endowed with wealth (of knowledge and achievements). It is common today to use "sir" to address persons with respect.

Shree Yantra

Shree Vidya is commonly worshipped not in the physical form as given above, but in form of a complex geometrical pattern called the Shree Yantra. This Yantra represents the scheme of creation in a miniature model. It is primarily made of triangles pointing upwards (representing the fire element), triangles facing downwards (representing the water element), circles (representing the wind element), squares (representing the earth element), and a dot in the centre (representing the space element). The Goddess is considered to be dwelling upon the dot. Other deities, representing key creative energies, dwell in their respective zones on the yantra. The lotus petals in the yantra represent the transcendental essence of life, and values like purity and positivism.

Mantra

In the mystical tradition of Tantra, while yantra is considered to be the abode of a deity, mantra is considered to be Her soul. Mantras are very powerful arrangement of letters and syllables, which has a complex phonetic design to connect individual consciousness to the Universal Consciousness. Mantra has a simple literal meaning, and a deeper intent it carries as a crucible of energy. It functions like a code word or password. Say your password is "ocean". When you type "ocean" in a given field, it does not mean literally 'a vast body of saline water". But, it actually means, "I, so and so, wish to access my site. Please allow me to do so." Here, "ocean" is a crucible for carrying a deeper, altogether different intent. Mantra-science was very well developed in ancient Vedic period. Recently, a great deal of research is taking place, as the Western world is waking up to the inherent possibilities of mantra-science.

Mantras must be pronounced with as much purity as is possible. It helps to understand the deeper meaning of a mantra, as it aids in fruition. However, even if the meaning is not understood, a mantra works as effectively. In fact, mystic tantric and shabar mantras have no "meaning" in the literal sense, but they are extremely effective.

Regular chanting of some mantras help alleviate stress and restore a sense of well being, apart from enveloping the individual with a flux of positive energy.

Pooja: Soulful Offerings

Significance of ritualistic worship

Ritual worship is an aid to connect with divinity. It helps our mind to gravitate and focus on the deity of worship. When mind is so centered on the deity, reflecting about the image and the divine deeds of the deity, it begins to imbibe similar positive energy, by means of spiritual osmosis.

Mythology and Folklore

History

Deepawali has been celebrated from ancient times in India, until today, in an unbroken tradition. It was a festival celebrated at the end of harvest season, when people shared the joys of bountiful produce amongst each other and by offering their worship to the Mother Goddess, the Goddess of Fertility. Even to this day, traditional businessmen close their books of accounts and celebrate their "harvest" of profits made during the year.

The Skandh, Padma, and Bhavishyat Puranas narrate the story of Maharaja Prithu, celebrating Deepawali as a fertility ritual. Some other texts refer to the *saagar manthan* , the Great Churning of the Ocean, and Goddess Lakshmee, the Goddess of Wealth appearing out of the churning. It indicates reward of labour by fruition of efforts (churning). Still other references are made to Lord Krishna liberating 16,000 young girls of Vrija (*gopis*) from the prison of the demon, Narakaasur, on this day. The Mahabharat narrates the story celebration of the Pandava princes returning home after an exile of 13 years.It reflects a similar, more popular, story of the Ramayana, where the return of Lord Rama with Sita and Lakshmana from their exile of 14 years is celebrated.

Sage Vatsayana, the author of Kama Sutra, refers to this night as Yaksha Ratri and calls the celebration as *"maahi maanya utsava"* . Al Beruni, the Persian historian who traveled through India in 17th century AD, records the celebration of the festival of lights. So did Nicolai Kanti, an Italian historian, note in his travel diary during his stay in India the 15th century AD. Abul Fazal, the historian during the reign of Akbar the Great, records the celebration as *"shab-e-raat"* in Ain-e-Akbari, and mentions that Deepawali festival enjoyed royal patronage and participation.

Ramayana

The Ramayana narrates the story of Lord Raama, believed to be an incarnation of Bhagwaan Vishnu. Some scholars-astrologers date the period of Raama to 9300 BC, based on the planetary configurations given by Sage Vaalmiki in his epic, the Ramayana. Shree Raama's father, Dasharatha, was forced to exile him for fourteen years. During this period, Demon Ravana, the King of Lanka, abducted Sita Devi, who was the wife of Shree Raama and was accompanying him in exile. Shree Raama fought a battle with Ravana, with the help of an army raised by Hanumaan, and other Vanara lords. A bridge was constructed across the sea from Rameshwaram, where Shree Raama worshipped Shiva, to Lanka. Rameshwaram is located at the southern tip of Tamil Nadu state in India. It is the pilgrimage of one of the twelve sacred jyotirlingas of Shiva. Recently, some satellite pictures released by NASA confirms the residue of a man made bridge submerged in the sea, located at the same place as it was built according to the mythology.

Ravana was vanquished. Peace and order was established in his kingdom. Shree Raama thereafter returned to Ayodhya, the capital of His kingdom, alongwith Sita Devi, his brother Lakshmana, and the chief of His allies, Hanumaan, and others. He was welcomed by His subjects amidst great celebrations. Ayodhya was lit with lamps. It was as if the Light of the land was returning after fourteen long years!

The Story of Bali

Sanatkumar Samhita narrates the story of Bali. Bali was the King of Demons. He had gained complete supremacy over all lands. He had captured the key deities, including Maa Lakshmee, and put them in prison. Bhagwaan Vishnu incarnated in form of a dwarf-child called Vaamana, and visited Bali. There, Bali, unaware of Vaamana's true identity, granted Him a gift of as much land as He could cover with His "three steps". Bhagwaan immediately assumed His mega-form. With one step, he covered all earth. With the second step, He covered all the creation above the earth. He asked Bali where should He put His third step. Bali, true to his word, offered his own head. Bhagwaan Vishnu, placed his third step on Bali's head, sending him to the nether worlds. He granted Bali liberation from the cycle of birth and death.

The deities were thus freed. There was celebration amongst gods. Maa Lakshmee granted boons of abundance to all, and proceeded to the Ocean of Milk, where She joined Bhagwaan Vishnu on His divine bed of serpents.

In some traditions therefore, a beautiful bed is laid out for Maa Lakshmee so that She may retire during the night, when She visits that home. In such homes, the family members do not sleep, but spend the night singing devotional songs, and performing elaborate rituals of worship. Advanced seekers perform spiritual practices during the night of Deepawali, seeking perfection in what they do.

The story also indicates that Bali was an atrocious king, who imposed heavy taxation. He collected all wealth from the people, and kept it in his treasury. In so much, he imprisoned Lakshmee, Goddess of Wealth, and kept Her captive, leaving his subjects in poverty. Lord Vishnu suppressed Bali, and released Lakshmee, by re-distributing the wealth equitibly.

Others

There are other mythologies around Deepawali. One is from the epic Mahabharata, where in Lord

Krishna narrates the story of Raajaa Mangala to Yudhishthira. It is about how Raajaa Mangala was led to worship Maa Lakshmee after facing devastation, and how with Maa's grace, he was restored to glory.

Almost every part of India, be it Kerala, Gujarat, or Kashmir, has its own Deepawali folk-lore, which is told and sung in groups in the villages.

Celebrations I

Rituals:

Preparing for celebration is an integral part of the ritual. Homes are cleaned up, uncluttered. A fresh coat of paint is put on the walls and doors. In most homes, walls are coated with lime. This acts an anti-insect and anti-bacteria coat. It is important especially as Deepawali is celebrated just after the rainy season, where in the insects increase in numbers manifold. In the villages, roofs are thatched with fresh straw obtained from the harvest.

The most common ritual for celebrating Deepawali is burning of lamps and playing with crackers. The temples, the cross-roads, and dark paths are also lit by lamps. As such, due to the rains, snakes and scorpions move around in the dark. The lights enable people to see them, and safeguard themselves. The light and the sound also represent the ritual of creation of the universe. It creates images that the Big Bang Theory of Creation also postulates.

People wear new clothes. New items of use or luxury are bought. Gifts are lavishly exchanged. Charity generously done. Traditionally, the businessmen used to close their books of accounts on this day. They would thank Goddess of Wealth for the profits, and for Her grace and blessings in enabling them earn their livelihoods. This occasion was used to renew personal bonds, settle old disputes, and start on a new slate. The act of being happy, being merry, and the process of celebration itself are the most sacred ritual of Deepawali.

Spiritual seekers do internal cleansing as a preparatory ritual. They work on their latencies and sub conscious mind, purging and purifying them. The night of Deepawali is considered as *siddha raatri* or the Night of Accomplishment. Seekers chant their guru-mantra, or perform advanced spiritual practices to kindle the inner Light and keep it ever aglow. Spiritually, all can celebrate the lighting up of our inner being by experiencing a gentle glow of Higher love and understanding, inside.

In medieval India, a king would collect several children from his kingdom. These children would be well fed, and given gifts. They would then be told to play amongst themselves. The kings was advised by the wise men to observe the children play. If the children chose to play with fire, it would be understood that an enemy may attack and burn the villages with fire. If the children played a war game, as soldiers, a war was thought to be imminent. If the children played with water, then good monsoon was expected. If the children sang songs, and danced, or narrated stories in turn, good times and many occasions to celebrate would be forthcoming. If the children played the game of marriage with dolls, there would be occasions of marriage in the royal household.

Associated Traditions/ Occasions

Dhanteras

(Two days before Deepawali, 13th day after full moon)

Dhanteras is celebrated two days before Deepawali. On this day, new utensils, or any other item of for house-wife, called the *Griha-Lakshmi* (Goddess of Home), is purchased. In the evening, a lamp filled with mustard oil is lighted and kept at the doorway. People clean their homes and belongings. The dirt is cast away. So is poverty, and all difficulties and obstacles. The stage is set for the welcome of *Dhana Lakshmi* (Goddess of Wealth).

Dhanteras is also considered to be the birth day of Dhanwantari, the ancient Vedic founder of the medical science, through the AyurVeda. This day is dedicated to re affirm ourselves to taking care of our health, by following the principles of positive and healthy living outlined in the Ayur Veda.

Roop Chaudas

(One day before Deepawali, 14th day after the full moon)

This day is dedicated to "roopa" ie Beauty. After health is beauty. This day is spent in taking care of one's beauty and form, by applying various fruit/

herbal packs on face and body. In modern times, a visit to the beauty parlour, or saloon would do!

Annakoot

(Next day to Deepawali)

This day is celebrated by preparing lavish food, offering the same to Lord Krishna, and distributing to the needy. This day celebrates the sacred act of sharing, we now call charity. Traditionally, people gather together with their food grains and vegetables. Various delicacies are cooked. In Uttar Pradesh, and some other parts of the country, fifty-six different dishes are prepared, and offered to the Lord. Then, there is a common feast, and community feeding.

It is believed that this day, Lord Krishna revealed His divinity by holding Mount Govardhan on the tip of His little finger, as all the people of Braja village gathered under the shade of the mountain, to be protected from the wrath of Indra, the Deity of Rains. Indra intended to drown all the people in rain, as they had stopped worshipping him. Govardhan is located near Vrindawan, 120kms from Delhi, and is a very sacred pilgrimage. People go around the mountain, saying their prayers. This circumbulation is stretched over 22kms.

Bhaiya Dooja

(Second day after Deepawali)

This day celebrates the love between sisters and brothers. Sisters pray for their brothers, and brothers in turn, get gifts for their sisters. Tradition has it that Yamuna, the Sacred River, prayed for her brother, Yama, the Deity of Death. Hence, this day is also called "*yama-dwiteeya*" . In Uttar Pradesh, where the river Yamuna flows for most part, brothers and sisters take a dip in Yamuna. Some flock to the Yama-ghaat, located on the banks of the Yamuna in Mathura, where it is believed that Yamuna prayed for the well being of her brother Yama. Yamuna had lost touch with her brother Yama, for a very long time. When Yama came searching for Her, He found Her at the Yama-Ghat (also known as Vishraam –Ghat). The sister was overjoyed to meet Him. She cooked His favourite dishes. Yama was pleased with His sister and granted Her a boon. She asked that those sisters and brothers take bath in the Yamuna at the Yama-Ghat, such brothers will not be troubled in Yama-loka, the Land of Dead.

This occasion enables women to keep in touch with their parental family, and be reassured that they are not left alone. It renews a sense of security, and a feeling of being cared for. Brothers being of the same generation, assure that the sisters will continue getting the same affection and support as always. The brothers visit the homes of their sisters, wherein they are able to assess the condition of their sisters, and understand their problems. If possible, the brothers (or, the elders) may take up difficult issues with the husbands' family and attempt to find a mutual solution.

Vishwa Karma pooja

(3 days after Deepawali)

This day celebrates the tools and equipment of livelihood. It is celebrated in more popularly in North, East and Central India. The tools and equipment are cleaned, and well oiled. Thereafter, these are worshipped. The presiding deity is Vishwa Karma, the Divine Architect. Factories are shut down. Self-employed people using tools also do not work on this day. The tools and equipment are allowed to be blessed and re energised by Vishwa Karma, so that they deliver required services for rest of the year.

Celebration II

Celebration of Light in other religious traditions

God is viewed as the Light in all major religious traditions of the world. In fact, such a view of God forms the substratum of the unifying streams of religious thoughts and beliefs. Light is therefore fundamental to most celebrations. Also, most meditative practices are woven around the vision of light.

Christianity

In Christianity, as in all religious traditions that believe in the Old Testament (like Islam and Zoroastrianism), God appeared in front of Prophet Moses in form of Fire. The 10 Commandments were delivered to Moses in that meeting. Jesus refers to God and even himself at times, as the Light. He said, "I am the Light" and later, "I and the Father in heaven, are one".

Christmas eve is celebrated in the night. Homes are lit up, so the Christmas tree. In the darkness of the night, the birth of Christ is celebrated. He is the Remover of all darkness. His birth ushers light. Burning candles in the church, or keeping the "light-vigil" are common Christian rituals.

Zoroastrianism

In the Jewish tradition, Fire- worship forms the central ritual of worship. Fire represents divinity.

Islam

In Islamic tradition, Allah is referred to as Noor-e-Illahi, the Light. It is common practice to light a lamp at the mosque, or on the graves of saints called Peer. Homes are decorated with lights on Eid.

Buddhism

Use of lamps in ritual-worship is key in Buddhism.

Jainism

Kalpasootra, a Jaina text, mentions that Lord Mahavira Jaina left is mortal body on this day. His disciples decided to celebrate this day, and remember Him in form of Light.

Fruition: The Fruits of doing Deepawali Pooja

Deepawali Pooja brings to us the grace of Goddess Maha Lakshmee. When the pooja is done with pure intent and devotion, one is blessed with health, wealth and prosperity. Obstacles to progress are removed. Negative planetary and stellar influences are reduced. Negative karmic burden is lightened. Mind and heart is filled with joy and positive energy.

On the night of Deepawali, a positive wave of spiritual energy flows across the world. By the process of ritual-worship, we partake of the positive energy by opening our individual subtle channels of energy to receive the Wave.

Deepawali pooja is an inspiration that stays even after the occasion. We are inspired to lead a positive life, and trust the love and grace of the Universal Mother. It also inspires us to clean up and un-clutter our external and internal environments.

List of items in the Offerings Deepawali Poojan-Paatra

List of Items to be arranged from a puja-shop

Some items of worship should be taken from the home. It brings in the collective-personal energy of the home and weaves the same into the ritual-worship. The following items are needed. They are commonly used in the kitchen, or easily procured from the grocery store.

Pictures of deities	as available in your temple/ home
Grains of rice	1 cup
Honey	3 tsp, keep in a cup/ bowl
Milk (Cow's preferably) (not boiled)	1 cup
Curd	1 cup
Water	1 jar (500ml)
Ghee (clarified butter)	2 tsp, keep in a cub/bowl

Sugar	3 tsp, keep in a cub/bowl
Fruits (5types)	4 bananas 2 apples 2 oranges 2 pears 100gms grapes (any fruit will do; even if only one variety of fruit is available, you may offer that with devotion)
Sweets	100gms or more (you may wish to cook rice-porridge with dry fruits at home)
Coconut (with water)	2 pcs
Clove (laung)	5 pcs
Cardamom (elaichi)	5pcs
Betel leaf (Paan)	2 leaves with stem (if possible/ available)
Grass (Doorvaa)	20 blades
Flowers	20 flowers or more
Flower petals	2 hands full
Leaves	1 small branch containing 3-5 leaves to put kalash
Currency coin	2 nos, 1 to be placed in the Kalash, 1 in the pooja as dakshina
Match Stick or lighter	1

Pooja-Plate	5 (a large steel/ silver/ metal plate would do. Else, use a large paper plate kept on another regular plate to prevent leakage of moisture dur ing pooja. Even a large leaf, like that of banana will do) 1 plate will be used to keep the yantra, and offer pooja 1 plate will be used to keep flowers, and rice 1 plate will be used to keep fruits and sweets 2 plates will be used to keep all the other ingredients (total 5 plates required)
Bowls (preferably metal)	6, one each for milk, curd, honey, ghee, panchamrita, and water
Small plates (3x3 inches)	6, one each for roli paste, sandal wood paste
Large lamp or bowl	1, to make a ghee lamp
Steel/ metal jar	1, to make a kalasha

Small spoons	6
Large spoons	2
Pooja seat	1, made of rug/ blanket well folded, covered with clean cotton bed sheet
Visitors' seat	as required
Tissue paper	1 box
Small towel	1 no.

CD player to play soft instrumental/ devotional music, if you desire

Deepawali - Poojan

Preparation

Plan to celebrate Deepawali, the festival of lights! Get into a positive and buoyant mood. Inspire your family and friends to join you for pooja. You can make it a family affair, or can invite friends to do a collective pooja. Let the family members be together for the pooja, and dinner thereafter. Stay together, unless there is an emergency preventing you from doing so. Even the sick members should be helped to be close to the pooja place, if possible. They should be cleaned (may be sponged) and changed into fresh, clean clothes, if possible.

Clean your house, if possible, the weekend before. Un-clutter your surroundings. At work too, un-clutter your drawer, clear up filing papers, and attempt to close pending issues.

Prepare the pooja place. Ideally, arrange for a sit-down pooja. It is possible to do pooja standing up, but that would be highly inconvenient, and tiring. A minimum space of

2 X 2 metres is needed to keep the pooja altar and seat two persons. You can choose the living room or any other room/ area for this purpose.

Make a nice altar on the table. Place the pictures of deities on it, after cleaning them. Decorate them with flowers. If there are children at home, they should help decorate the deities and the area around. You can use paper/ plastic articles, or balloons to bring about a festive mood. Turn on all lights in your house, so that every corner is lit, and darkness banished.

Keep all the articles/ items needed for pooja near the pooja altar. Take the items from the Offerings Deepawali Pooja-Paatra and keep them in a plate so that you can clearly read the labels on each item. It will help you in getting the item when needed during pooja.

It is advisable that while doing pooja, let another person role play /officiate as the reader-priest. Request your child/ spouse/ friend to help you with this.The reader should slowly read the mantras from the book, and you should repeat after him/ her. This person can also help you with passing on items you would need during the pooja. In case you are alone, you should read the mantras slowly, and follow the instructions. Maintain a poise of devotion and joy while doing the pooja.

Before starting the pooja take bath. Change into clean (or new) clothes. Clothes must be loose and comfortable. Avoid black and blue colour. Red, maroon, yellow, saffron, even green colours are considered auspicious. These colours represent positive energy, from spiritual point of view. In India traditionally, women wear as much jewelry as possible, and dress up well, as if the highest dignitaries are visiting them on Deepawali. Indeed, the deities are in no way less!

Prepare the Kalash

1. Tie mauli around the neck of the jar.
2. Pour some water in a jar. Put a little Ganga jal in it.
3. Put the following items in the jar:
   One currency coin
   Panch ratna
   Sarvaushadhi
   Sapta mritika
4. Place the leaves around the mouth of the jar.
5. Tie mauli around a coconut. Place the coconut on the mouth of the jar.
6. Spread jau grains where you intend to keep the jar (kalasha) near the altar.
7. Now place the jar on top of the jau grains.

Prepare the main Lamp

You may either have the lamp at home already, or you can make it by taking a steel bowl and filling it with ghee (clarified butter). Make a thick cotton wick by rolling a strip of cotton on your palm. Put the cotton wick in the bowl. In case it is not possible, then light a candle.

Place a lamp at the pooja altar.

Pooja-plate

Take a large plate. With your finger dipped in roli paste, make a swastika/ om (in hindi/ sanskrit)/ or just a dot at the centre of the plate.

Keep the plate down in front of you. All pooja will be done in this plate.

Wash the Shree Yantra (copper yantra/plate) with water. Place the same in the plate. Next to it, place one Supari (beetel nut), preferably in the standing position, with its broad bas down, and the pointed top facing upwards.

Prepare Panchamrita

Take a bowl.

In it, put 11 tsp of milk, 3 tsp of curd, 1 tsp of ghee, 1 tsp of honey, and 1 tsp of sugar. Mix all of these properly with a spoon.

Others

Put the sandal wood powder in a small bowl. Pour little water in it and make a paste.

Similarly, make a paste of roli powder.

Take 5 tsp of rice grains. Put 3 tsp of water and make it wet. Mix some flower petals and a little roli paste in it.

Take a bowl and put water in it. Put a little Ganga jal in it. Place a small spoon in the bowl.

Keep milk, curd, ghee, honey in different bowls with a small spoon in each of them.

Switch off or turn off the volume of your mobile phones and house phones. In case you are expecting any emergency/ important call during the time of pooja, delegate the task of answering the calls to some one around you. In case it is unavoidable to refuse the call or you are alone, try to be as brief as possible, if you do get a call during the pooja.

Also, avoid jokes/ fun/ gossip during the course of the pooja. You can have fun while preparing for the pooja, and even afterwards. But again, avoid idle gossip/ criticism/ negative speech/ anger.

Depute someone to help fetch an item in case you need it during the pooja, and did not keep it during the preparation for pooja.

Precautions

Go about doing the process of doing the pooja with a calm and rested mind. Do not be in a rush, as that may create unnecessary anxiety. Be careful when you use knife to cut the fruits. Or when you burn the lamps or the incense. Ensure that the lamp is not kept on anything inflammable, like paper or cloth.

Switch off the fan in the vicinity of the pooja altar to prevent the lamps from extinguishing. When pouring water or carrying it, be careful not to spill the same. After the pooja, thoroughly clean the pooja place so that no residue of grains, or sugar or other items remains on the ground.

Wash your hands after doing the pooja so that any residue of roli, sindoor or other colours are washed away. Do wash your hands before eating prasad, in case you would hold the prasad or eat it with bare hands.

Mantra : How to pronounce correctly

It is very difficult to pronounce Sanskrit words that comprise the mantras. It has been attempted in this book to transliterate the mantras from Sanskrit to English in such a manner that it is easy to pronounce. The words have been split into easy syllables, and spelt so that an individual can follow and pronounce. You should read slowly, or ask someone else to read and you repeat after him/ her. The mantras are written in italics. In smaller font, the meaning and intent of mantras, wherever necessary, has been mentioned. You can say the meaning aloud after reading the mantra, if you wish to.

a= is pronounced as "*a*" as in c*a*ll

aa= is pronounced as "*aa*" as in f*a*ther

ee= is pronounced as "*ee*" as in tr*ee*
oo= is pronounced as "*oo*" as in s*oo*n
sh= is pronounced as "*sh*" as in *sh*oot
ch=is pronounced as "*ch*" as in *ch*ance
gh=is pronounced as "*gh*" as in "a*gh*ast"

FAQs (Frequently Asked Questions)

When can I do Deepawali Poojan?

Deepawali Poojan should be started within one hour of sunset, ideally. But in different parts of the world, the time of sunset varies vastly. We suggest doing the Deepawali Poojan starting between 5.30pm to 8.00pm, depending on individual convenience.

Do I need to take bath before doing Deepawali Poojan?

Bath helps to physically cleanse you of sweat and dirt. It also cleanses your body of negative static electric charge that your body gathers during the day, due to rubbing of the clothes, or the wind against your body. Experientially, it makes you feel fresh, relaxed and positive. It is recommended that you take bath. However, you may choose not to.

Do I have to wear fresh clothes?

As in the case of bath, so in the case of fresh clothes. Fresh clothes induce relaxation, joy, and positive spirit. For pooja, clothing should be loose and comfortable. Kurta- pyjama, lungi-kurta, and dhoti-kurta are ideal Indian dresses for men. Salwar-kurta (avoid tight churidaar type salwar), and sarees are good for women. Both can wear loose T-shirts and track pants, or any other dress you feel comfortable in. Clothing should ideally be washed, and not torn from anywhere.

Do I need to be fasting, before doing Deepawali Poojan?

No, you do not need to be fasting before doing Deepawali Poojan. It is recommended that you may avoid eating a very heavy meal at least one hour before doing the pooja. Heavy meal causes physical and mental sluggishness, which hinders the process of offering your best emotions to Goddess. You can sure have a light and snacks and tea before doing pooja, if that makes you feel better and well grounded. Those who smoke, should do so before hand, so that the urge to smoke does not distract you during pooja. It is recommended that you do not consume alcohol, or alcoholic beverage just before doing the pooja. It is also recommended that you avoid non-vegetarian food on the day of Deepawali, all meals if possible, or at least dinner after the pooja. Eggs are considered non-vegetarian for this purpose.

Can I use the washroom (toilet) during the pooja?

It is also recommended that you use the washroom before starting the pooja, so that the pooja is not interupted. However, if you have to use the wash room in between, then do so. Wash your hands and face. Start the pooja with first chanting the mantra for purification "pavitrikaranam" which is chanted at the beginning of the pooja. Then mentally bow down to your Guru, Ganesh jee, and Maa Maha Lakshmee, seeking their blessings in order to continue. Thereafter, continue from where you paused before going to the wash room.

Where in home can I do Deepawali Poojan?

You should ideally do pooja at the temple-altar in your home, where you keep the picture of the deities normally. Some people have a room for this, some others keep the pictures in a cupboard in their rooms or in the kitchen. There should be sufficient place for you to sit or stand in front of the altar, and for your family to be present. There should be place to keep the pooja plate. You can place a small table or stool in front of the altar for this purpose.

You can also choose to do pooja in your living room, or any other room convinient to you. You can set up a small temple on a table. Cover the table with a clean table cloth. Place the picture of deities you have at home, after cleaning them. Place a vase of fresh flowers on the table. Use your imagination to decorate, with fruits, flowers, leaves, etc. Place your pooja seat in front of the temple, and make space for other members of the family to be seated too.

After the pooja, on the next morning, keep the pictures of the deities back to where they were kept before.

How should my pooja-seat be (aasana) ?

Your seat should be comfortable, yet firm. Avoid very soft cushions, as they tend to give you back aches. Use a firm cushion. Or spread a rug or a blanket folded to size . Cover it with a clean cotton bed sheet. If possible, use red, yellow, saffron or white colours. Avoid the use of blue and black colours.

Other people who would join you for pooja should also have comfortable seats to sit down.

In case you have a difficulty in sitting on the floor cross-legged, you may use a high cushion to raise your hips, so that your knees touch the ground. You may even use a low height stool or chair. You should be seated comfortably, and should be able to keep your spine straight. Avoid slouching.

Can I use utensils from my kitchen for the pooja?

Yes you can use utensils from your kitchen for the pooja. Make sure they are washed clean, and not used for by anyone just before the pooja, in which case, clean it again. Say, you are using a glass to keep water for pooja, and someone drinks from the glass just then. You should wash the glass, before using it for pooja again.

Can I use items and ingredients like rice grains, sugar, milk etc from my kitchen from the containers these are regularly kept for daily use?

Yes you can use the same ingredients for pooja. Avoid using half-eaten, half-used items, like a banana, which has been eaten partly by someone or sugar which has been kept in a sugar pot served with tea, from which people consumed sugar, and possibly used tea-dipped spoon to serve it.

If I do not pronounce the mantras correctly, will they still be effective? Will faulty pronunciation make me incur sin?

Yes, the mantras will be effective, any which way. The core strength of the mantra is the intent of the person who chants it and the essence which the mantra embodies.

"bhaavey hi devaah vasati"- the deities dwell in the emotion with which the mantra is said.

The following story illustrates this point. Vaalmiki was an uneducated robber. Seven-Sages met him and transformed his heart and mind. They initiated him with the mantra "*Raama*", and instructed him to repeat the mantra till Bhagwaan Raama blessed him. Vaalmiki immediately proceeded with his penance and chanting. But by an error of understanding, he chanted the opposite of "*raama*", ie, "*maraa, maraa, maraa...*" (meaning "the dead one"!). However, his pure intent and devotion got him the blessings of Bhagwaan Raama. Vaalmiki went on to write the great epic called The Raamaayana.

There is no sin incurred by faulty pronunciation of mantras. However, it is true that there are some advanced mantras, which loose their efficacy if not chanted properly. The mantras in the Deepawali Pooja-Vidhi are of general nature, and do not loose their efficacy or cause any sin if not chanted properly.

If you have the time and inclination to do so, please read aloud the translation in English after each mantra. This will amplify your intent and help you focus your attention on the deeper essence of the mantra.

What do I do, if I do not understand some instruction, or do not know what to do with some ingredient/ item of pooja?

If you do not understand a step in the pooja, just skip it, and go to the next. If you do not understand what you need to do with some ingredient, just offer the same in the pooja-plate, with great devotion and love.

What do I do, if I am unable to arrange for some ingredient of pooja?

In place of such an ingredient that you could not arrange for, use rice and petals of flowers. In case you cannot arrange for flowers, use rice. Mix rice with turmeric powder and roli, and use this mixture.

Is playing dice/ gambling, a necessary ritual of Deepawali?

No, playing dice and gambling is in fact prohibited. Rig Veda 10/34/13 instructs "*aksheerma deerya*" meaning, "Do not play dice". Bhavishyat Purana, (Part-II, Chapter4) and Padma Purana (Chapter-122) defines *Dhyoot Kriya* (gambling) as detrimental to prosperity, and ethics.

Manusmriti (Chapter-9, Shloka-223), and Narad Smriti clarifies by categorising gambling into two types, viz- *jihwaa-kaarit* and *samaahavya* . The first type is detested and banned. The second type is encouraged.

The first type is typical gambling/ betting "by tongue" (*jihwaa-kaarit*). This kind of game is played out of indolence and extravagance. It does not respect the value of wealth, earned through right means and hard work. It promotes whimsical behaviour, and over dependence on chance or destiny, making people fatalistic in their approach. It causes strife, and disharmony between losers and winners.

The winner takes it all, and the loser has to fall in disgrace. The epic of Mahabharata describes how even the wise, like Yudhishthira, betted and lost his kingdom, his brothers and even his wife Draupadi in a game of dice. It led to the ruin of all.

For the sake of pure entertainment, with very minimal stakes, one can play dice. The stakes should not be in any case more than what one would part with to a beggar. Say Rupees 10, in India, or a dollar or a pound equivalent, overseas! With low financial stakes or a funny stake like the loser having to act like a clown, dice becomes a game of harmless fun and mutual camaraderie.

The second type is profound speculation, "by considering pros and cons"(*samaahavya*).

A few days before Deepawali, as a part of the celebration, men would get into speculating the harvest, or the strength of the horses, or the value of the cows. There would be horse racing, cattle-fair, and even sports like wrestling. Such speculation depended on knowledge of the macro and micro economy, weather conditions, breeding history of the animals, and bio-cultural background of wrestlers. Soldiers were recruited/ promoted, horses bought for the army, and trade, and cattle –milch cows and oxen for agriculture and transportation were traded. In modern times, speculating in stocks or promoting sports are similar activities. Such type of "*dhyoot kriya*" was allowed.

Part II Deepawali Poojan - Vidhi

(Laghu Pooja)

(May take 15-25 minutes to perform)

Mangalaa charanam (Prayer for Auspicious Grace)

मंगलम् भगवान् विष्णुः मंगलम् गरुरध्वजः
मंगलम् पुण्डरीकाक्षय मंगलाय तनो हरिः।

सर्व मंगल मंगल्यै शिवे सर्वार्थ साधिके
शरण्यै त्र्यम्बके गौरि नारायणि नमोस्तुते।

Fold your hands, meditate on Lord Vishnu and Maa Durga Devi, and say:

mangalam bhagwaan vish nuh mangalam garura dhwaja
mangalam pundari kakshay mangalaya tano harih

sarva mangal mangalayei shivey sar vaarth saadhikey
sharanyei triam bakey gauri naraayani namastutey

Lord Vishnu is Auspicious, His flag, which bears the picture of Garuda, the eagle, is also auspicious, His lotus like eyes are auspicious, He is Auspicious, He is remover of all evils.

Shivey (Maa Durga) is Auspicious and giver of all things auspicious. She fulfills all (legitimate) desires. We seek refuge in Your loving grace, Oh Maa Gauri. You are the Triad of forms and creation. We bow down to You, Maa Naaraayani

Lighting of Main Deepak (Lamp)

You may either have the lamp at home already, or you can make it by taking a steel bowl and filling it with ghee (clarified butter). Make a thick cotton wick by rolling a strip of cotton on your palm. Put the cotton wick in the bowl. In case it is not possible, then light a candle.

Place a lamp at the poojaa altar. Light it carefully with a match stick or candle stick. Take a flower and some rice in your hand, meditate on the Light and its guiding spirit and say:

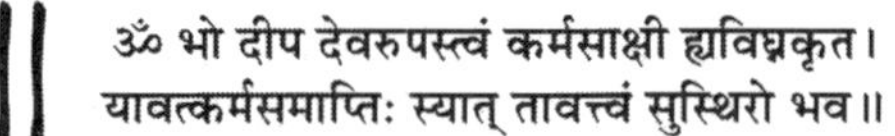

om bho deep devah upas twam karma saakshi hya vighna krita
yaa vad karma samaap tihi syaata taa vad twam su sthiro bhava

Oh Deva in form of the Lamp (Deep Devah), please bless us by your presence. Please witness the offerings of our worship (and so convey to the respective deities). Please remove all obstacles in performing the worship. May we please request You that until the worship is completed, You please be unwavering (and in Your presence may our minds become unwavering, not- disturbed and distracted; may we be like Your steady flame, in mind and spirit)

Disha Bandhanam (Protection from Evil)

Whenever any auspicious task is undertaken, whether worship or work, anti-waves of distracting elements emerge from any and all directions. In order to maintain focus of mind and intent of purpose, it is important that we shield ourselves from all distractions by making a firm resolve to that effect. Above all, we should seek the protection of the Divine Mother, Maa Durgaa.

Meditate on being in the protective embrace of Maa, and seek Her strength to strengthen yourself.

Take yellow mustard seeds in your left palm and cover with your right hand. Say the mantra below. Pick a pinch of these and sprinkle in all the directions around you, above you and on the floor.

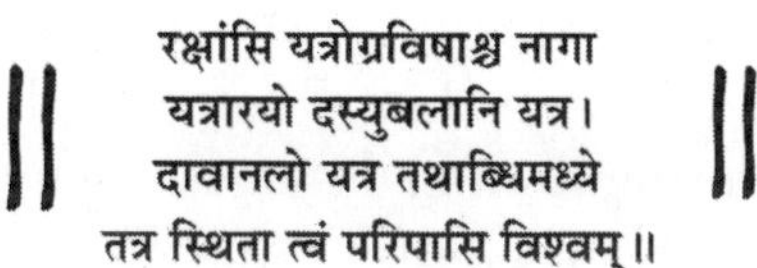
रक्षांसि यत्रोग्रविषाश्च नागा
यत्रारयो दस्युबलानि यत्र।
दावानलो यत्र तथाब्धिमध्ये
तत्र स्थिता त्वं परिपासि विश्वम्॥

rak shaansi yatro gra vishash cha naa gaa
yatraa rayo dasyu balaani yatra
daavaa nalo yatra tathaa abdhi madhye
tatra sthitaa twam pari paasi vishwam

Protect me, Maa, from poisonous serpents (in form of wicked men, and thoughts; poisons in form of toxins and diseases that over power our bodies and cause decay; poisons also in form of words of anger that we spew at each other), powerful robbers (cheats, in form of men, and internally in form of delusions of our minds), fierce fires (of unforeseen adversities, of raging flames of insatiable, unending desires that lead us away), waters (that flood and destroy, like emotions and thoughts that often drown us), in such or any circumstances, may I be protected in by Your presence, even as you protectively hold the world.

Guru Pooja

Guru, (Master/ Teacher), is the most important entity in our life. He imparts knowledge, which differentiates between animals and us human beings. His blessings are sought before any act. This enables us to align our deeds on knowledge-base, rather than based on whims and impulses. Those who have a guru may meditate on him. Those who don't have a guru may meditate on Light streaming upon you as the grace of Divine Guru.

Take some rice and flowers in your hands and say:

|| गुरुर्ब्रह्मा गुरुर्विष्णुः गुरुर्देवो महेश्वरः।
गुरुः साक्षात् परंब्रह्म तस्मै श्री गुरवे नमः॥ ||

om gurur brahmaa gurur vish nuh
gurur devo mahesh varah
guru reva param brahma
tas mai shree guruve namah

Place the rice and flowers in the pooja-plate, and fold your hands.

Guru is Brahma (the Creator, as he creates a new human being out of us, by means of imparting knowledge to us of the Real and the Unreal, and revealing to us the true purpose of our lives), Guru is Vishnu (the Sustainer, as he sustains our existence on this planet by navigating us on our true path), Guru is Maheshwara (Shankara, the Destroyer, as he destroys all ignorance, so that creation/ revelation of knowledge occurs), Guru alone is the Absolute Brahman (the Highest Truth, as he leads us to the realisation of our oneness with God). I bow down to such Guru.

Pavitrikaranam (Purification)

Purity is Divinity. Purity of thoughts, words and action precede any sacred act, like worship. Meditate upon a gentle shower of rain drops infusing a sense of joy and optimism in you (taking away the impurity of gloom and distress). Meditate on the rain shower washing the environment around you- the flowers and leaves, the trees and the land, every blade of grass getting bathed in purity.

Take a spoon of water and pour it in the cup of your right palm. Cover it with your left palm. Say :

ॐ अपवित्रः पवित्रो वा सर्वावस्था गतोऽपि वा।
यः स्मरेत पुण्डरीकाक्षं स वाह्याभ्यन्तरः शुचिः॥

om apavitrah pavitro vaa sarvaa vas thaam gatopi vaa
yah smareta pundari kaak sham sa
vaahya abhaya antarah shu chih

Sprinkle the water on yourself and around you.

May the water purify wherever it reaches.

I meditate on the Lotus Eyed, Bhagwaan Vishnu, Whose grace purifies me, both externally and internally, physically, mentally, emotionally and spiritually. Like the lotus is ever pure, even though born out of, and rooted in the mud; like the leaves of the lotus are never wet, even though they are always in water, so also, with a purity of vision and perception, I see only purity around, and become pure (Lotus-Eyed)

Aasan shuddhi (Purification of the Seat of Pooja)

The seat upon which we sit down has to be firm and comfortable (sthiram sukham aasanam- yoga sutra, in reference to our posture- physical, emotional, mental and spiritual.) The seat upon which our consciousness rests, in as much as the seat on which our body rests, should be pure, firm and pleasant. Aasana, at deeper levels also stands for our core values upon which we firmly build our lives.

Seeking purification of our being, as well as our worship seat, take a pinch of rice and petals, put it under your worship seat. Then take kusha, and put this also under your worship seat. Touch the seat with your right hands and say:

ॐ पृथ्वी त्वाया धृता लोका देवित्वं विष्णुना धृता।
त्वं च धारय मां देवि पवित्रं कुरू चासनम् ॥

om prithvi twayaa dhritaa lokaah devi twam
vishnu naa dhritaa
twam cha dhaa raya maam devi pavi tram kuru cha aasa nam

Oh Mother Earth! You uphold all Life! Goddess, You also uphold Lord Vishnu (and, thus all creation). Please hold me too (in your lap), and may You purify my worship seat.

Aachmanam (Holy Sip of Water of Life)

Water is life. Most of our bodies, 96% or more, is essentially water. In the Gita, Bhagwaan Krishna says, "Of water, I am the sapidity, (rasoham apsu)".

Meditating upon the sacredness and purifying energy of water, take a spoon full of water with your left hand and pour into your right palm, folded as a cup. Say the first mantra and sip the water. Again take water, say the next mantra and sip.

ॐ केशवाय नमः

om kesha vaaya namah (sip the water)

I bow to Keshava, the One Who Rests in Water, Who is the Giver of Water of Life to all beings.

ॐ नारायणाय नमः

om naaraa yanaaya namah (sip the water)

I bow to Naaraayana, the Field of Knowledge, from Whom we derive all that we know .

ॐ माधवाय नमः

om maadha vaaya namah (sip the water)

I bow to Maadhava, the Sweetness of Bliss, Who grants everlasting peace and happiness.

Now, take water again in your right palm, say the mantra below, and drop the water on your left side, as if washing your hand.

ॐ हृषीकेषाय नमः

om hrishi keshaaya namah
(drop water on your left, as if washing your hand)

I bow to Hrishikesha, the Lord of Senses, Who grants sensual pleasure, and restrain thereof.

Tilak Dhaaranam (Tikka)

Tilak is a mark put on the forehead, just above the point where the eyebrows meet. About 5 cms inside from that point lies the pitutary gland, also called the Master Gland. The Pitutary gland controls all vital bodily functions. It is also considered as the seat of the Soul- our consciousness, in fact our very being. The Aagyaa chakra is also located in this region, as is the mystical "Third Eye of Wisdom and Intuition".

Meditating on the Third Eye, take sandal paste with the tip of your right-hand's ring-finger, and put the same on your forehead. Say:

चन्दनस्य महत्वंपुण्यं पवित्रं पापनाशनम्।
आपदं हरते नित्यं लक्ष्मी तिष्ठतु सर्वदा॥

chanda nasya mahat punyam pavitram paap naash nam
aapadaam hara tey nit yam lakshmee vasati sarva daa

Sandalwood has great merits. It purifies, and destroys all evils. It always takes away troubles, and Goddess Lakshmee ever dwells with it.

Sandalwood gives fragrance and coolness. It is believed that even ordinary trees around a sandal tree become similarly fragrant. Venomous snakes coil around the sandal tree trunk, and lie intoxicated. The fragrance of positive values, attitude and behaviour can intoxicate any one who comes in our circle of influence, and can turn animosity into amiability. As such, all wealth dwells with such a person.

Sarvadeva Namaskaaram (Offering of Obesience to Main Dieties)

Mix rice, roli, petals and little water. Take a small pinch of this mixture and sprinkle in the pooja-plate at the end of each mantra. Then take another pinch of the mixture and sprinkle at the end of the next mantra. Meditating on the respective deities as mentioned in the brackets respectively, take a pinch of the mixture and say:

ॐ श्रीमन्महागणाधिपतये नमः।

om shree man mahaa ganaa dhi pataye namah
(I bow to Lord Ganesha)

ॐ लक्ष्मीनारायणाभ्यांनमः।

om laxmi naaraa yanaa bhyaam namah
(I bow to Lakshmee- Vishnu)

ॐ उमामहेश्वराभ्यांनमः।

om umaa mahesh waraa bhyaam namah
(I bow to Paarvati- Shiva)

ॐ वाणीहिरण्यगर्भाभ्यां नमः।

om vaanee hiranya garbhaa bhyaam namah
(I bow to Saraswati- Brahma)

ॐ शचीपुरन्दराभ्यां नमः।

om shachi puran daraa bhyaam namah
(I bow to Shachi-Indra)

ॐ मातृपितृ चरणकमलेभ्यो नमः।

om matri pitri charan kama lebhyo namah
(I bow to the lotus feet of my parents)

ॐ इष्टदेवताभ्यो नमः।

om ishta devetaa bhyo namah
(I bow to my personal deity)

ॐ ग्राम देवातभ्यो नमः।

om graam devetaa bhyo namah

(I bow to the deity of this city)

ॐ वास्तु देवताभ्यो नमः।

om vaastu devetaa bhyo namah
(I bow to Vaastu Devataa)

ॐ सर्वेभ्यो देवेभ्यो नमः।

om sarve bhyo devey bhyo namah
(I bow to all deities)

ॐ सर्वेभ्यो देवेभ्यो नमः।

om sarve bhyo braah maney bhyo namah
(I bow to all the learned men)

॥ ॐ सिद्धि बुद्धिसहिताय
श्रीमन्महागणाधिपतये नमः। ॥

om sidhdhi budhdha sahitaaye
shree man mahaa ganaa dhi pataye namah
(I bow to Lord Ganesha, accompanied by Siddhi (Accomplishments), and Buddhi (Intellect).

Shree Ganesh-Lakshmi Pooja

Take a pinch of rice and a few petals of flowers in your hands and meditate on Lord Ganesha and Maa Paarvati. Seeking their presence during worship, say:

॥ ॐ श्रीगणेशम्बिकाभ्याम् नमः।
ध्यान् आवाह्यनम् समर्पयामि॥ ॥

om shree ganesha ambikaa bhyam namah
dhyaan aavaahanam samarpaayami

Place the rice and petals on the supaari (betel nut)

Kalash Pooja (The Divine Container)

Take a pinch of rice and a few petals of flowers in your hands and meditate on the Kalasha as the Space that contains all Creation, and the deities that dwell there in. Seeking their presence during worship, say:

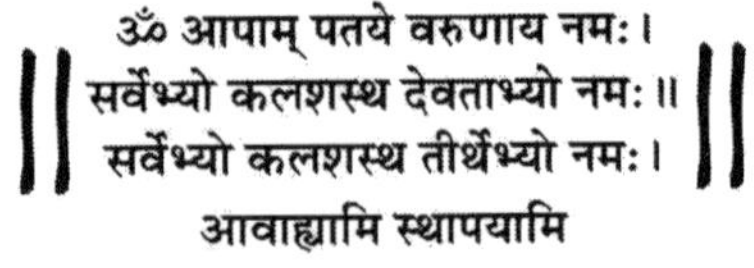
ॐ आपाम् पतये वरुणाय नमः।
सर्वेभ्यो कलशस्थ देवताभ्यो नमः॥
सर्वेभ्यो कलशस्थ तीर्थेभ्यो नमः।
आवाह्यामि स्थापयामि

om aapaam pataye varunaaye namah
sarvey bhyo kalash astha devtaa bhyo namah
sarvey bhyo kalash asha teerthey bhyo namah
avaahyaami sthaapayaami

Place the rice and petals on the Kalasha

I bow to the Lord of Waters, Varuna. I bow to all the deities who dwell in the Kalasha. I bow to all the holy rivers that dwell in the Kalasha.

Shodash Maatrikaa Poojanam

There are 16 creative deities in the Vedic liturgy. They are responsible for the process of creation through progressive differentiation of elements and energies.

Meditating on the 16 –Mothers or creative deities, take rice, petals, and fruit (coconut, if available) in your hands. Seeking their presence during worship, say:

|| ॐ गणेश साहित गौर्यादि षोडष्मात्रिकाभ्यो नमः ।
षोडष्मात्रिकाये नमः ध्यान आवाह्मम् समर्पयामि ॥ ||

om ganesha sahita gaur yaadi shodasha matrikaa bhyo namah
shodash maatri kaaye namah dhyaan aavaa
hanam samar payaami

Place rice and petals on the supaari (betel-nut) in the pooja- plate.

I bow to Lord Ganesha, Maa Gauri, and other 16- Cosmic Mothers

Navagraha Poojanam

There is an intricate inter-dependence and control between us as individuals (microcosm) and the universe (macrocosm). The movement of the Sun controls our external environment, causing day and night, seasons to change, and life itself to be sustained. The Moon controls our internal environment, our minds, our moods, our response to the external environment apart from our psychosomatic health. Other planets too influence our lives at subtle levels. These planets reflect energy waves upon us, from distant constellations. Our energies are deeply inter woven with that of the universe, much more than we are consciously aware of. Scientific research is progressively taking our knowledge of such matrix to newer frontiers.

Meditating on the 9 planets-deities, take rice and petals in your hands. Seeking their presence during worship, say:

ॐ ब्रह्मा मुरारिस्त्रिपुरान्तकारी भानुः शशी भूमिसुतो बुधश्च।
गुरुश्च शुक्रः शनिराहुकेतवः सर्वे ग्रहाः शान्तिकरा भवन्तु॥

om brahmaa muraari tripu raanta kaaree
bhaa nuhu shashee bhoomi suto budhash cha
gurush cha shukrah shani raahu keta wah
sarvey grahaah shaanti karaa bhavantu

सर्वेभ्यो सूर्यादि नवग्रहा देवताभ्यो नमः।
ध्यान् आवाह्नम् समर्पयामि।।

sarve bhyo sooryaa di nava grahaa devataa bhyo namah
dhyaan avaa hanam samar payaami

Place rice and petals on the supaari (betel-nut) in the pooja- plate.

I bow to Brahma, Vishnu and Shankara. They the Triad called GOD- Generation (Creation), Operation(Sustenance) and Destruction (Change). I bow to the Sun, the Moon, the Son of Earth (Mars), Mercury (the Giver of Intellect), Jupiter (the Master-Teacher), Venus (the Illumined, and the Illuminator), Saturn (the Slow paced Giver of Results), Rahu (the Dragon's Head) and Ketu (the Dragon's Tail). May all planet-deities be appeased and bless me with peace.

Shankha-Ghanta Poojanam (Conch Shell- Poojaa Bell)

Shankha or Conch Shell was blown as a victory sound in battles or upon start or completion of an important task like worship or yagya. Ghanta or the Metal-Plate gong too used to be hit to create a deep metallic sound on similar occasions. Even to this day shankh and ghanta are used to create sound on auspicious occasions. Sound is a primordial energy. It is considered to be more basic than light. The "Big Bang Theory" postulates the release of enormous energy in the form of sound at the beginning of the creation. The Bible too mentions "In the beginning there was Word (sound)."

Meditating on the Sound energy emanating from the conch shell and gong, take rice and petals in your hands. Seeking the presence of the deities that dwell there in during worship, say:

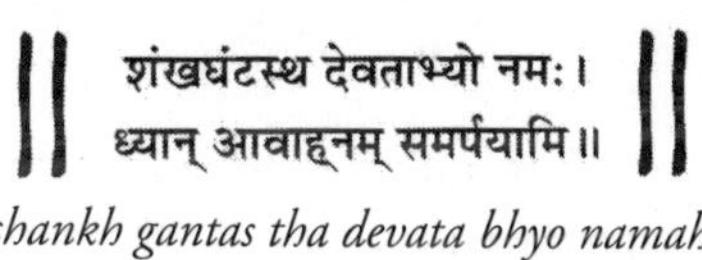
|| शंखघंटस्थ देवताभ्यो नमः।
ध्यान् आवाहनम् समर्पयामि॥ ||

shankh gantas tha devata bhyo namah
dhyaan avaa hanam samar payaami

Place rice and petals on the supaari (betel-nut) in the pooja- plate.

Shree Vidya Maa Maha Lakshamee Pooja (on the Shree yantra)

Maa Maha Lakshmee is the presiding deity of Deep-aawali Poojaa. She is also known as Shree Vidyaa, Shree Tripura Sundari, or simply Shree. This is also a title prefixed before every male name in India. For married women, Shreemati is prefixed to their names. Shree stands for wealth- material and spiritual. Shree Vidya Maa Mahaa Lakshmee is the bestower of all wealth. She is the primordial Cosmic Mother, the Creatrix. It is with Her spur that Shiva, so far just a "shava" (corpse; Pure Pontential), becomes Shiva. Together they unfold the entire Cosmic creation.

Dhyanam

Meditating on the Mother Maa Maha Lakshmee take a pinch of rice and petals in your hands. Seeking Her presence during worship, say:

|| या देवी सर्वभूतेषु लक्ष्मीरूपेण संस्थिता।
नमस्तस्यै नमस्तस्यै नमस्तस्यै नमो नमः॥ ||

yaa devee sarva bhootey shu lakshmee roo pena sans thitaa
namas tasye namas tasye namas tasye namo namah

|| ॐ महालक्ष्म्यै नमः।
ध्यान आवाहनम् समर्पयामि॥ ||

om mahaa lakshmyai namaha
dhyaana avaa hanam samar payami

Sprinkle rice and petals on the shree yantra in the pooja-plate.

To the Devi, Goddess, who dwells in all creation in form of Lakshmee,

I bow, I bow, I bow and I surrender

Praan Pratishthaapanam (Offering Life-Force, Praana)

Meditate on the Mother, Maa Maha Lakshmee and all the other deities so far invoked. With the intent of infusing them with life by offering a speck of your own life, take a pinch of rice and petals in your hands, say:

|| ॐ गणेशाम्बिकादि सहितं सर्वेभ्यो
आवाहित प्रतिष्ठित देवताभ्यो नमः
ततः प्रधान देवता महालक्ष्मी देव्यै नमः
सु प्रतिष्ठा वरदा भवन्तु ||

om ganesha ambikaa di sahitam sarvebhyo
aavaa hit devataa bhyo namah
tatah pradhaan devata mahaa lakshmi devye namah
su pratish thaa vardaa bhavantu.

Sprinkle rice and petals on the shree yantra in the pooja-plate.

I bow to Lord Ganesha, Maa Paarvati, along with all the invoked deities and the presiding deity Maha Lakshmee. May they all be infused with life, and bless me with their glorious presence.

The following is offering of courtesies to the deities invoked.

Aasanam (Offering seat to Dieties)

Take a pinch of rice and petals, say the mantra and sprinkle on the shree yantra in the pooja-plate.

आसनम् समर्पयामि।

aasanam samar payaami

I offer my heart as your throne and foot stool, Oh Goddess and all Deities invoked!

Paadhyam (Offering water to wash feet)

Take a spoon full of water, say the mantra and put on the shree yantra in the pooja-plate.

पाद्योः पाद्यम् समर्पयामि।

paad yoho paad yam samar payaami

I wash Your lotus feet with the waters of my emotions

Arghya (Offering water to wash hands)

Take a spoon full of water, say the mantra and put on the shree yantra in the pooja-plate.

हस्तौः अर्घ्यम् समर्पयामि।

hast yoho argh yam samar payaami

I wash Your divine hands with the waters of my devotion.

Aachamanam (Offering water to wash mouth)

Take a spoon full of water, say the mantra and put on the shree yantra in the pooja-plate.

मुखे आचमनीयम् जलम् समर्पयामि।

mukhey aach manee yam jalam samar payaami

I wash Your beautiful mouth with the waters of my love

Snaanam (Offering water to bathe)

Take a spoon full of water, say the mantra and put on the shree yantra in the pooja-plate.

स्नानम् जलम् समर्पयामि।

snaa nam jalam samar payaami

I bathe Your celestial body with the waters of my life

Panchaamrita Snaanam (Offering special bath :milk, curd, ghee, honey, sugar)

Milk represents nourishment. Curd stands for change- the only unchanging law of life. It represents transformation, and evolution. Ghee stands for fuel of the fire of life. Honey represents the fruition of labour. It is the extract of the essence of goodness that is present in different flowers. It has healing energy too. Sugar represents sweetness in all thoughts, words and action. Sweetness makes life a pleasant experience.

Take a spoon full of panchamrita, say the mantra and put on the shree yantra in the pooja-plate.

पंचामृत स्नानम् समर्पयामि।

pancha amrita snaanam samar payaami

I bathe You with the Elixir- grant me immortality (in terms of understanding and legacy of good deeds).

Shuddhodaka (Offering fresh water bath)

Take a spoon full of water, say the mantra and put on the shree yantra in the pooja-plate.

शुद्धोदक् जल स्नानम् समर्पयामि।

shuddh odaka jala snaa nam samar payaami

Vastram (Offering cloth)

Clothing offers protection. By offering symbolic protection, we seek divine protection.

Take a piece of mauli, 3 inches long, say the mantra and put on the shree yantra in the pooja-plate.

वस्त्रम् समर्पयामि।

vastram samar payaami

Aachamanam (Offering fresh water)

Take a spoon full of water, say the mantra and put on the shree yantra in the pooja-plate.

आचमनीयम् समर्पयामि।

aacha manee yam samar payami

Yagyopaveetam (Offering sacred thread- janeyu/ yagyopaveeta)

The sacred thread stands for responsibility. It is a pair of threads, each of three rounds. The knot itself is made in five rounds. It represents the responsibilities arranged in 3s and 5s. Eg. 3s are the thought, word and action. 5s are the 5 sense organs and 5 organs of action. We bestow our responsibility on the deities by offering the sacred thread.

Take the sacred thread, say the mantra and put on the shree yantra in the pooja-plate.

यज्ञोपवीतम् समर्पयामि।

yagyo pavee tam samar payaami

Aachamanam (Offering fresh water)

Take a spoon full of water, say the mantra and put on the shree yantra in the pooja-plate.

आचमनीयम् समर्पयामि।

aacha manee yam samar payami

Upa Vastram (Offering the minor clothing)

Take a piece of mauli, 3 inches long, say the mantra and put on the shree yantra in the pooja-plate.

उपवस्त्रम् समर्पयामि।

upa vastram samar payaami

Aachamanam (Offering fresh water)

Take a spoon full of water, say the mantra and put on the shree yantra in the pooja-plate.

आचमनीयम् समर्पयामि।

aacha manee yam samar payami

Chandanam (Offering sandal wood paste)

Take a little chandan paste with a petal, say the mantra and put on the shree yantra in the pooja-plate.

चंदनम् समर्पयामि।

chanda nam samar payaami

Akshatam (Offering rice, unbroken pieces)

Rice stands for the water element at the subtle level, transformed into nourishment. Unbroken pieces of rice (akshata) stand for firm resolve, and unbroken promises. While we seek to obtain divine promises of support, we also offer our promise to do our humble bit in life.

Take a pinch of rice, say the mantra and put on the shree yantra in the pooja-plate.

अक्षतान् समर्पयामि।

aksha taan samar payaami

Pushpam (Offering a flower)

Flower stands for the earth element at the subtle level. It also represents the dynamic process of action, which later leads to fruition. We offer all our actions to the Divine in form of a flower. May our actions be as beautiful, as effortless, as perfect, as fragrant, as tender and as complete as the flower we offer.

Take a flower, say the mantra and put on the shree yantra in the pooja-plate.

पुष्पम् समर्पयामि।

push pam samar payaami

Doorvaa (Offering blades of grass)

Grass represents fertility and growth. It also represents humility, and utility of the highest order. It stands for ability to withstand adversity. May we learn from the humble blades of grass.

Take a few blades of grass, say the mantra and put on the shree yantra in the pooja-plate.

दूर्वांकुरान समर्पयामि।

doorva anku raan samar payaami

Sugandhit Dravyam (Offering fragrance-essence of flowers, Itr)

Fragrance represents the earth element. It is the subtlest part of a flower, yet its very identity and fundamental intent. Fragrance travels against the breeze. Hence it represents upholding our core values even in face of trials and adversity.

Pour a little itr on a petal, say the mantra and put on the shree yantra in the pooja-plate.

सुगंधित् द्रव्यम् समर्पयामि।

sugan dhit drav yam samar payaami

Sindoor (Offering sindoor)

Sindoor is made of mercury and sulphur fused together as mercuric sulphide. Mercury represents the essence of masculine energy which is cool and watery. Sulphur represents the essence of feminine energy, which is hot and fire-like. Sindoor represents the process of becoming one of the two polarities of energy, the yin and the yang, the light and darkness, the pure potential and the dynamic, and such like. Sindoor is therefore worn as a mark of marriage by most Hindu women in the parting of their hair or as a round mark on their forehead. It represents the creative force through unison of energies. We seek the creative force to play in our lives by offering sindoor.

Take a little sindoor on a petal, say the mantra and put on the shree yantra in the pooja-plate.

सिंदूरम् समर्पयामि।

sindoo ram samar payaami

Naanaa Parimal Dravyam (Offering variety of elements-roli, abir, gulal, haldi)

Take a pinch of each of the above- roli, abir, gulal, haldi (turmeric tuber), jayphal, karjamba, and lotus seeds. Say the mantra and put on the shree yantra in the pooja-plate, one by one.

नाना परिमल द्रव्यम् समर्पयामि।

naanaa parimal dravyam samar payaami

Dhoopam (Offering Incense)

The smoke emanating from the dhoop and incence represents the air element. Air represents breath. It also represents the vital process of differentiation beginning the space element which differentiates into air, then fire, water and finally earth, the grossest element of creation. Air represents movement and change. It also stands for ultimate flexibility and ability to blend. It assumes the shape of the container it dwells in. May we accept, and be accepted in all situations of life. May we accept changes, and change seem-lessly, when needed to.

With your hands, wave the smoke of the dhoopam towards the pooja-plate, and say the mantra.

धूपम् आघ्रयामि।

dhoo pam aaghraa payaami

Deepam (Offering the Light)

The Flame of light represents the fire element. It sustains praana, the life-force that flows in within us in subtle channels (called naadis). It is replenished through breath. The fire element causes the sense of sight and speech to function, as well as the metabolic function in the human body, which is essential to burn glucose and release its subtle content – energy. Fire also represents the all consuming energy that reduces all things to ashes, releasing the subtle contents into the universe. Fire sacrifice, known as yagya, is integral part of vedic ritual. It is also a part of Jewish tradition of worship. In the Christian and Islamic tradition which follow the Old Testament, God reveals Himself to Moses in form of fire. We offer the fire element, seeking divine warmth and guidance (light) as we traverse our paths on this planet.

With your hands, wave the light of the lamp towards the pooja-plate, and say the mantra.

दीपम् दर्शयामि।

dee pam darsha yaami

(Take a spoon full of water, and wash your hands on your left side)

Naivedyam (Offering the fruits)

Food satiates hunger, by nourishing our body and pleasing our senses. The food is consumed by the five primary life forces in our body. They are called praana, apaana, vyaana, samaana, and udaana. We offer food, so that we are abundantly satiated, that we never hunger.

Take pancha mewa(dry fruits) and a piece of sweet, say the mantra and put on the shree yantra in the pooja-plate.

|| नैवेद्यम् निवेदयामि क्षुधातृप्तिार्थे
नैवेद्यम् समर्पयामि। ||

naivey dyam niveda yaami kshudha tripti arthey
naivey dyam samar payaami

ॐ प्राणाय स्वाहा।

om praa naya swaa haa

ॐ अपानाय स्वाहा।

om apaa naaya swaa haa

ॐ व्यानाय स्वाहा।

om vyaa naaya swaa haa

ॐ समानाय स्वाहा।

om samaa naaya swaa haa

ॐ उदानाय स्वाहा।

om udaa naaya swaa haa

Jalam (Offering fresh water)

Take a spoon full of water, say the mantra and put on the shree yantra in the pooja-plate.

|| पुनः हस्तमुखप्रक्षाल्यार्थे जलम् समर्पयामि। ||

punah hasta mukha prak shaalya arthey jalam samar payaami

Udwartanam (Offering of cleansing)

Udwartana is also called ubtan in common Hindi. It is used to deeply cleanse the skin. Brides and grooms are applied ubtan as a ritual just before marriage. It signifies cleansing of all deep seated dirt from the past, enabling us to move forward in life with a "clean skin". May we be cleansed from the dark shadows of our past.

Take a little sandalwood paste on a petal, say the mantra and put on the shree yantra in the pooja-plate.

उद्वर्तनार्थे गंधम् समर्पयामि।

udwar tana arthey gandham samar payaami

Ritu phalam (Offering of seasonal fruit)

Fruits represent the space element. Space contains all. The fruit contains the seeds, which in turn contain not only a tree, but the possibility of infinite number of forests. The fruits of our actions contain infinite possibilities of consequences. We, therefore, offer the fruits of our actions to the Divine Mother. She, in Her supreme compassion and love for us, will allow only beneficial consequences to materialise for us, thus we pray.

Take a seasonal fruit or a banana, say the mantra and put on the shree yantra in the pooja-plate.

ऋतु फलम् समर्पयामि ।

ritu phalam samar payaami

Mukh shuddhi (Offering of mouth freshner)

At times, what we eat leaves a bad odour and taste in the mouth. A mouth freshner cleanses the breath, and makes it pleasant. The exhaled breath does not disturb others with bad odour. The exhaled breath also represents spoken words. A fresh mouth should speak pleasant words. Lord Jesus Christ said that a man is defiled not so much by what goes into his mouth, but by what comes out of it. Foul breath can be corrected by mouth freshner. Foul words can leave deep, indelible marks. May we become aware of the words that leave our mouth. May our words be as fragrant as the mouth freshner.

Take a clove, cardamom, and betel leaf (paan) (if available), say the mantra and put on the shree yantra in the pooja-plate.

|| एला लवंगादि सहितम्
ताम्बूल पत्रै समर्पयामि। ||

elaa lawanga aadi sahitam taam bool patram samar payaami

Akhand Shree Phalam (Offering of coconut)

Coconut represents a human head. When skinned of all fibres, spots resembling eyes, nose and mouth can be seen. We offer our ego as a coconut, as an act of complete surrender to the Divine Mother.

Take a coconut, say the mantra and put on the shree yantra in the pooja-plate.

अखण्डश्रीफलम् समर्पयामि।

akhanda shree phalam samar payaami

Dakshinaa dravyam (Offering of wealth)

A spec of our earning is offered, seeking abundance of wealth

Take a coin (dollar/cent), say the mantra and put on the shree yantra in the pooja-plate.

दक्षिणा द्रव्यम् समर्पयामि।

dak shinaa drav yam samar payaami

Prayer

Take a pinch of rice and petals, say the mantra and put on the shree yantra in the pooja-plate.

॥ ॐ गणेशाम्बिकादि सहितं सर्वेभ्यो
आवाहित् प्रतिष्ठित् देवताभ्यो
नमः। ततः प्रधान् देवता महा लक्ष्मी देव्यै नमः॥ ॥

Om ganesha ambikaa di sahitam
sarvebhyo aavaahit pratishthit devataa bhyo namah
tatah pradhaan devata mahaa lakshmi devye namah

I bow to Lord Ganesha, Maa Paarvati, along with all the invoked deities and the presiding deity Maha Lakshmee.

Ashta lakshmi poojan

Maha Lakshmee has 8 primary forms, called Ashta-Lakshmee. Each represents a distinct energy of wealth, without which what we refer to as wealth is meaningless.

Mix rice, roli, petals and little water. Take a small pinch of this mixture and sprinkle on the shree yantra in the pooja-plate at the end of each mantra. Then take another pinch of the mixture and sprinkle at the end of the next mantra. Meditating on the respective deities as mentioned in the mantra respectively, take a pinch of the mixture and say:

ॐ आद्यलक्ष्म्यै नमः ॥१॥

om aadyaa lakshamyee namah

I bow to the Goddess of Primordial Wealth, the source of all wealth.

ॐ विद्यालक्ष्म्यै नमः ॥२॥

om vidyaa lakshamyee namah

I bow to the Goddess of Wealth of Knowledge, which creates and keeps all wealth.

ॐ सौभाग्यलक्ष्म्यै नमः ॥३॥

om sau bhaagya lakshamyee namah

I bow to the Goddess of Wealth of Good Fortune, which enables us to strike gold.

ॐ अमृतलक्ष्म्यै नमः ॥४॥

om amrita lakshamyee namah

I bow to the Goddess of Wealth of Elixir, that preserves and protects till eternity

ॐ कामलक्ष्म्यै नमः ॥५ ॥

om kaama lakshamyee namah

I bow to the Goddess of Wealth of Desire, which stokes the passion to possess and enjoy.

ॐ सत्यलक्ष्म्यै नमः ॥६ ॥

om satya lakshamyee namah

I bow to the Goddess of Wealth of Truth, which leads to self-realisation, our highest human need.

ॐ भोगलक्ष्म्यै नमः ॥७ ॥

om bhoga lakshamyee namah

I bow to the Goddess of Wealth of Indulgence, which enables us to enjoy what we have.

ॐ योगलक्ष्म्यै नमः ॥८ ॥

om yoga lakshamyee namah

I bow to the Goddess of Wealth of Yoga, which unites our consciousness with Divinity.

Kuber poojan

Meditate on Yaksha Raaja Kuber, the Keeper of Celestial Wealth.

Take a pinch of rice and petals, say the mantra and put on the shree yantra in the pooja-plate.

ॐ कुबेराय नमः

om kuberaaya namaha

Dawat Pooja (Books of Accounts/ Pen) (optional)

Place the inkpot in front of the altar.Tie the mauli (red thread) around it. Put a tilak on the bottle, and some rice and petals. Say:

ॐ श्री महाकाल्यै नमः

om shree maha kaalyee namaha

Now tie mauli around the pen, put a tilak on it, sprinkle some rice and petals on it and say:

ॐ लेखनी स्थायै देव्यै नमः

om lekhinee sthayee devyee namaha

Take the cash book/ dairy/ notebook, and make a swastika on it or just a tilak with roli, or paste of chandan powder and saffron. Meditate on Goddess Saraswati, the Goddess of Learning. Sprinkle rice and petals on it and say:

|| ॐ वीणापुस्तकधारिण्यै श्रीसरस्वत्यै नमः ||

om veenaa pustaka dhaarinyee shree saraswatyee namaha.

Show incense and lamp to the ink-pot, the pen and the notebook just now worshipped.

Deepa maalikaa poojan (the lamps)

(In case you have several lamps to be lit, for decorating your house)

Place 3,5,7,9,11, or more earthen lamps in a plate. Fill the same with ghee (clarified butter) Fill one lamp with til(seasme) oil/ mustard oil/ any vegetable oil. Place think cotton wicks in each of the lamps. Light all of them. Say:

ॐ दीपमालिकायै नमः

om deepaa valyee namaha

Place some rice grains, and juicy whole fruit (orange, etc) next to the plate containing lamps. Fold your hands and offer your respect to the lamps, seeking them to light up all darkness, and, illumine and lead you on the right path in life

After the pooja, place these lamps at the main door of your house, or other places around your house as you wish to.

Aarti

Take a small steel plate (copper/ brass/silver would also do). Place a very small bowl in it. Take a piece of camphor and light it with a lamp, then place in the bowl. Or, place the piece of camphor in the bowl and light it with a burning matchstick, lighter, or candle. Hold the plate with your right hand and offer the camphor-flame to dieties by swaying the plate gently in front of the pooja- plate. In case the camphor is about to burn out, put more pieces of camphor into the bowl. Other members of the family/ friends who are present, and wish to perform aarti can do the same with the aarti plate, and say the same mantra as given below. You may stand up, and bend down, if you wish. Say the mantra:

|| कर्पूरगौरं करुणावतारं संसारसारं भुजगेन्द्रहारम्
सदा वसन्तं हृदयार्विन्दे भवं भवानी सहितं नमामि। ||

karpur gauram karunaa vataaram
sansaar saaram bhujagendra haaram
sada vasantam hridayaa ravindam
bhavam bhavaani sahitam namaami

Fair as camphor, Maa Paarvati, and compassion incarnate, Shiva,

The essence of creation, Maa Paarvati, and adorned with the garland of serpents (Energy), Shiva, May you ever dwell in the lotus abode of my heart.Oh! Shiva-Paarvati, in form of Bhavam, Pure Potential, and Bhavani, Dynamic Energy! I bow down to You!

Keep the aarti plate down. Take a spoon of water. Make a circle over the plate with the water filled spoon. Pour the water in front of the pooja-plate on the ground. Say:

आआर्तिक्यम् समर्पयामि।

aar aartikyam samarpayaami

I offer aarti to You

You may cup your palms over the flame and then caress your forehead and face with your palm, as if to spread the warmth of blessings thus obtained. Other persons present may do the same.

Pushpaanjali (Offering of flowers)

All family and friends present at the poojaa should take petals of flowers in their hands and say:

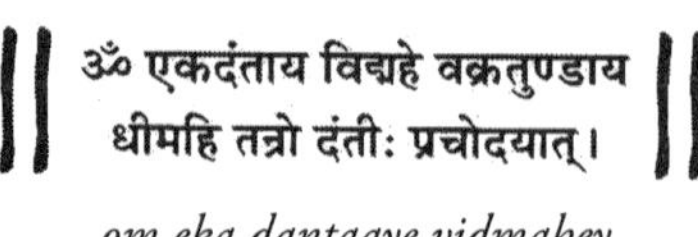
|| ॐ एकदंताय विद्महे वक्रतुण्डाय
धीमहि तन्नो दंती: प्रचोदयात्। ||

om eka dantaaye vidmahey
vakra tundaaye dheemahi
tanno dantihi prachodayaat

Ganapati Gayatri: I meditate on the One-Toothed Lord, whose trunk is bent. May He lead and guide me.

ॐ महालक्ष्म्यै च विद्महे विष्णु पत्न्यै च
धीमहि तन्नो लक्ष्मीः प्रचोदयात्।

om mahaa lakshamaye cha vidmahe
vishnu patnaye cha dheemahi
tanno lakshmihi pracho dayat

Lakshmee Gayatri: I meditate on Mahaa Lakshmee, who is the consort of Bhagwaan Vishnu. May She lead and guide me.

त्वमेव माता च पिता त्वमेव त्वमेव बन्धुश्च सखा त्वमेव।
त्वमेव विद्या द्रविणं त्वमेव त्वमेव सर्वं मम देव देव॥

twameva maataa cha pitaa twameva
twameva bandhush cha sakhaa twameva
twameva vidya dravinam twameva
twameva sarvam mam deva deva

You alone are the Mother and the Father, Your are the Family and the best Friend. You alone are the Knowledge, You alone the Wealth, You alone are my All, Oh God! Oh Mother!

नानासुगन्धपुष्पाणि यथाकालोदभवानि च।
पुष्पांजलिम् मया दत्ताम् गृहाण परमेश्वरः

naanaa sugandhi push paani yathaa kaalod bhavaani cha
pushpaan jalim mayaa dattam grahaan parmesh warah

I offer flowers of various fragrances gathered in my palm to You, Maa Bhavaani! May You please accept my humble palm-full of floral offerings.

ॐ गणेशाम्बिकादि सहितं सर्वेभ्यो आवाहित् प्रतिष्ठित्
देवताभ्यो नमः। ततः प्रधान् देवता महा लक्ष्मी देव्यै नमः॥

om ganesha ambikaa di sahitam
sarvebhyo aavaahit pratishthit devataa bhyo namah
tatah pradhaan devata mahaa lakshmi devye namah

I bow to Lord Ganesha, Maa Paarvati, along with all the invoked deities and the presiding deity Maha Lakshmee.

Offer the petals of devotion to Maa Mahaa lakshmee.

Pradakshina (circumbulation)

Meditate on the wheel turning around the axis. Meditate on Goddess as the axis, and you wrapping around Her feet, or simply turning around Her as a wheel. Meditate on the Wheel of Life, the Wheel of Time, the Wheel of Good Fortune, turning around Mother

Goddess. Stand up and turn from your left to your right in clockwise direction. Make 3 rotations. Say:

ॐ यानि कानि च पापानि ब्रह्म हत्या समानि च
तानि तानि प्रणश्यन्ति प्रदिक्षणा पदे पदे ॥

om yaani kaani cha paapani
brahma hatyaa samaani cha
taani taani pranayashanti
pradakshiney padey padey

Whatever sins I have committed, even the most grim and ghastly, may each be destroyed with each step of my circumbulation. May I be purified, and reshaped by Goddess, as fresh clay on potter's wheel is transformed into a beautiful piece of pottery, having lost all impurities it had as mud.

Shaanti Paath (Prayers for Peace and Happiness of All Beings)

Meditate on a wave of peace spread over the entire world. All present may say;

तमसो मा ज्योतिर्गमय असतो मा सद्गमय
मृत्योर्मामृतम् गमय। ॐ शांति : शांति : शांति : ॥

tamso ma jyotir gamaya
asato ma sad gamaya
mrityur ma amritam gamaya
om shantihi shantihi shantihi

From darkness (of ignorance), take us to light (of knowledge),

From untruth (of seeking fulfillment in the temporary world), take us to Truth (of self-realisation, and source of all fulfillment),

From death(of our bodies), take us to immortality (realisation of our immortal Self, the Soul)

May there be peace, may there be peace, may there be peace!

Kshama Prarthana (Offering apology and seeking forgiveness)

Meditate on the Mother Goddess and seek Her loving forgiveness for any fault in performing Her ritual worship. In fact, every deed of ours, every act is our offering to Her. Errors should be recognised, rectified and never repeated. That is true repentance. Maa's grace and forgiveness is reflected in our actions becoming closer to perfection. Fold your hands and say:

|| आवाहनं न जानामि न जानामि विसर्जनम्।
पूजां चैव न जानामि क्षम्यतां परमेश्वरि॥ ||

aavaa hanam na jaanaami na jaanaami visar janam
poojaam chaiva na jaanaami kshama sva param eshwari

मन्त्रहीनं क्रियाहीनं भक्तिहीनं सुरेश्वरि।
यत्पूजितं मया देवी परिपूर्णं तदस्तु मे॥

mantra heenam kriyaa heenam bhakti heenam suresh wari
yat poojitam mayaa devi pari poornam tadastu mey

I know not how to invite You, Maa, nor how to bid You farewell

Nor do I know how to offer You my prayers, please forgive Oh Goddess!!

My worship has been with impure mantras, rituals, and devotion.

Please make them complete and pure, and accept them yet as mine!!

Dedication

We offer the dedication of our worship to Bhagwaan Vishnu. Meditate on V   Vishnu and say:

कायेनवाचा मनसेन्द्रियेर्वा
बुद्धात् मनवप्रकृतेः स्वभावात्
करोमि यद् यत् सकलम् परस्मै
नारायणायेति समर्पयामि।

kayen vaacha manas endriyair va
budh dhyat mana va prakriteh sva bhaavaat
karomi yad yat sakalam paras mai
naaraa yanaa yeti samar payaami

Whatsoever I perform with my body, words, mind or senses Or intellect or nature, I dedicate to Bhagwaan Naaraayana

Visarjan (Conclusion of the Pooja)

Meditate on all the deities being thanked and bid farewell to. Place your hand gently over the yantra and the supari in the pooja-plate. Say:

gachcha gachcha sur sreshthey swa sthanam parmeshwari
poojaa raadhan kaale cha punaraa gamanaaya cha

Gently shake the supari and the yantra and also the kalasha, as if all deities are leaving. Take a spoon of water and put under your worship seat, touch the floor with the tip of your fingers and touch your forehead thereafter.

Oh Foremost amongst Deities! May You depart and reach Your abode, Goddess!

Whenever I invoke You for worship, please do come again and bless me with Your presence.

Raksha Sootra Bandhanam (Tie mauli)

Ask someone to tie mauli (red thread, also called kalava). Mauli has to be tied on your right wrist. Take a pinch of rice and flowers in your right hand and clench your fist closed. Keep the palm side facing downwards, while mauli is being tied. Then, put the rice and petals in the pooja-plate. Thereafter, you may tie mauli to all present in a similar manner. You may also put tilak on everyone's forehead.

While tying mauli, meditate on divine protection and say:

|| येन बद्धो बली राजा दानवेन्द्रो महाबलः।
ते नत्वांपतिबध्नामि रक्षे माचल माचल ॥ ||

yen baddho bali raaja daanava endrom mahaabalah
tey natwa manu baghnaami rakshey maachala maachala

The protective thread that was tied on the most mighty King Bali, I tie on you too, so that you are ever protected.

Prasada (The Blessings)

Now, distribute sweets and fruits as prasada (the pleasure and blessings of Goddess) to all present. Give with your right hand, into their right hands. Joyfully eat and celebrate!

Daana (Offerings to Charity)

There is a universal law- you reap what you sow, you get what you give. If you need a tree, you need to plant only a tiny seed. If you need a harvest of crops, you need to sow a few seeds, plant a few saplings. If you need love, you have to give love. If you need respect, you have to give respect. Similarly, if you need wealth, you have to give away wealth selflessly to charity. Deepaawali being a festival of Goddess of Wealth, Maa Mahaa Lakshmee, you have prayed for Her to bless you with wealth. It would be beneficial if you take out some money and send to charity of your choice.

Offerings India supports Sadhuwan Foundation. Your donations will be gratefully accepted. It will be used towards building the temple of Goddess Mahaa Lakshmee Shri Vidya, along with the Centre of Silence for meditation and spiritual education, located at Voda Mahadev temple, Noida, India. Sadhuwan Foundation has other social initiatives like health education in the villages around the temple, and primary medical care. There is a gurukul that teaches vedic sciences to young children from the village.

If you so wish, you may send your donation to
Sadhuwan Foundation
A-81, Sector-26, NOIDA-201 301 (UP)
India

Tying the Prosperity Knot

Let the pooja-plate remain as is for the whole night.

Next morning, after taking bath, take the red cloth and spread it. Pick the following from the pooja plate and keep in it.

Shree yantra (Some may want to keep the shree yantra in their pooja altar)

Pieces of turmeric

Blades of grass

Yellow mustard seeds

Dollar coin

Supari

Lotus seeds

Jay phal

Few petals of flowers

Show incense to these. Then tie a gentle knot with the red cloth, so as to secure all of these items within the knot. Hold in your hands, meditate on the blessings of wealth that you have received, and say:

|| ॐ यद् बधनन् दाक्षायना हिरण्यशतानीकाय सुमनस्यमानाः ।
तन्मा बंधामिशतशारदाय आमुष्यज्ञं दष्टिर्थसम् ॥ ||

om yadaa badhanan daakshaayanaa hiranya
shataa neekaaya sumanasya maanaah
tanma aa bandhaami shata shaardaaya
aamushyanja dashtir thaa sam

Keep this bundle in your cash box, or the place where you keep money.

I tie this knot to contain the wealth that gives

me a pleasant and balanced mind and intellect. May prosperity remain ever lasting (a hundred autumns) and may it give me health, wealth, happiness and fame.

Nirmaalya (pooja residue)

The left over of the pooja may be suitably disposed. In various traditions, it is disposed differently. It may be put in the garden under a tree, put in flowing water, put in a heap and burnt, or put in a plastic disposal bag and kept in the bin. Please note that after the pooja is done and the deities have been sent away, the pooja residue is like any other left over, and can be disposed accordingly.

Mantra Japa, and Meditation (optional)

The night of Deepaawali is considered very auspicious for performing deeper spiritual practices, as learnt from qualified Masters (Gurus). Those of you who chant specific mantras or do special practices, may wish to take out sometime around mid night to sit in meditation and perform those practices. For those of you who do not have any specific mantra to chant, yet may want to practice on Deepaawali night, the following simple mantra and practice may be performed.

1. Sit comfortably, with your back firm and straight. You may sit cross-legged on a soft

seat put on the floor, or may sit on the edge of a chair, with your spine straight. Keep your hands in your lap, or on your knees, palm-side up. Keep your eyes gently closed.

2. Relax your forehead, your face, your shoulders, your back and full body.

3. Breathe evenly, with your stomach rising and falling.

4. Draw your attention to your breath. ONLY OBSERVE your breath. DO NOT CONTROL your breath. Observe as the breath enters your nostrils, touches the skin, travels deep in. Observe as the breath leaves the nostril, to return again.

5. Stabilise your breath. Breathe gently. Do not use force. Do not break your breath, either when you breathe in or when you breathe out.

6. When your mind is calm and reasonably composed, gently begin to chant any one of the following mantras for as long as you wish, without counting:

ॐ नमः शिवाय।

om namah shivaaya

|| हरे राम हरे राम राम राम हरे हरे
हरे कृष्ण हरे कृष्ण कृष्ण कृष्ण हरे हरे ||

hare raama hare raama raama raama hare hare
hare krishna hare krishna krishna krishna hare hare

ॐ ऐं ह्रीं क्लीं चामुण्डायै विच्चे।

om ain(g) hreen(g) kleen(g) chaamun daayee vichhey

Part III Deepawali Poojan - Vidhi

(Brihat Pooja)

(Time Needed: 60-75 minutes)

Mangalaa charan (Prayer for Auspiciousness and Grace)

मंगलम् भगवान् विष्णुः मंगलम् गरुरध्वज
मंगलम् पुण्डरीकाक्षय मंगलाय तनो हरिः ।

सर्व मंगल मंगल्यै शिवे सर्वार्थ साधिके
शरण्यै त्र्यम्बके गौरि नारायणि नमोस्तुते ।

Fold your hands, meditate on Lord Vishnu and Maa Durga Devi, and say:

Mangalam bhagwaan vish nuh mangalam garura dhwaja
Mangalam pundari kakshay manga laaya tano harih

Sarva mangal mangalyee shivey sar vaarth saadhikey
Sharanyee triam bakey gauri naaraa yani namas tutey

Lord Vishnu is Auspicious, His flag, which bears the picture of Garuda, the eagle, is also auspicious, His lotus like eyes are auspicious, He is Auspicious, He is remover of all evils.

Shivey (Maa Durga) is Auspicious and giver of all things auspicious. She fulfills all (legitimate) desires. We seek refuge in Your loving grace, Oh Maa Gauri. You are the Triad of forms and creation. We bow down to You, Maa Naaraayani

Lighting of Main Deepak:

You may either have the lamp at home already, or you can make it by taking a steel bowl and filling it with ghee (clarified butter). Make a thick cotton wick by rolling a strip of cotton on your palm. Put the cotton wick in the bowl. In case it is not possible, then light a candle.

Place a lamp at the poojaa altar. Light it carefully with a match stick or candle stick. Fold your palms together, meditate on the Light and its guiding spirit and say:

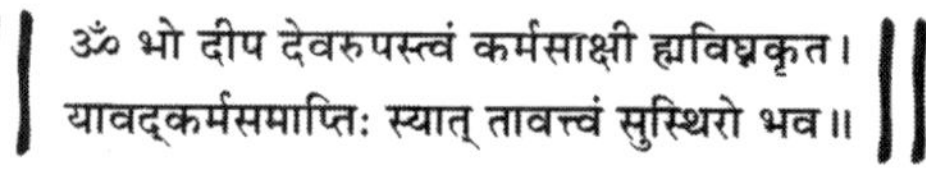
ॐ भो दीप देवरुपस्त्वं कर्मसाक्षी ह्यविघ्नकृत।
यावद्कर्मसमाप्तिः स्यात् तावत्त्वं सुस्थिरो भव॥

Om bho deep devah upas twam karma saakshi hya vighna krita
Yaavad karma samaap tihi syaata taavad twam susthiro bhava

Oh Deva in form of the Lamp (Deep Devah), please bless us by your presence. Please witness the offerings of our worship (and so convey to the respective deities). Please remove all obstacles in performing the worship. May we please request You that until the worship is completed, You please be unwavering (and in Your presence may our minds become unwavering, not- disturbed and distracted; may we be like Your steady flame, in mind and spirit)

Dishaa Bandhanam (Protection from Evil)

Whenever any auspicious task is undertaken, whether worship or work, anti- waves of distracting elements emerge from any and all directions. In order to maintain focus of mind and intent of purpose, it is important that we shield ourselves from all distractions by making a firm resolve to that effect. Above all, we should seek the protection of the Divine Mother, Maa Durgaa.

Meditate on being in the protective embrace of Maa, and seek Her strength to strengthen yourself.

Take yellow mustard seeds in your left palm. With your right hand, pick a pinch of these and say the mantra below. Sprinkle in the direction mentioned at the end of each mantra. Then take a pinch of seeds again, and say the next mantra. So on till the end.

|| त्राहि मां देवि दुष्प्रेक्ष्ये
शत्रूणां भयवर्धिनि। ||

traahi maam devi dush prekshey shatroo naam bhaya var dhini

प्राच्यां रक्षतु मामैन्द्री

praachyaam rakshatu maam endree (EAST)

आग्नेय्यामग्निदेवता

aagney yaam agni devataa (SOUTHEAST)

दक्षिणेऽवतु वाराही

dakshineya vatu vaaraahee (SOUTH)

नैर्ऋत्यां खड्गधारिणी

naiy rityaam khadaga dhaarinee (SOUTHWEST)

प्रतीच्यां वारुणी रक्षेद्

pratee chyaam vaarunee rakshed (WEST)

वायव्यां मृगवाहिनी

vaaya vyaam mriga vaahinee (NORTHWEST)

उदीच्यां पातु कौमारी

udee chyaam paatu kaumaaree (NORTH)

ऐशान्यां शूलधारिणी

aishaa nyaam shoola dhaarinee (NORTHEAST)

ऊर्ध्वं ब्रह्माणि

urdhwam brahmaani (UPPER REGIONS- SKY)

मे रक्षेदधस्ताद् वैष्णवी तथा

mey rakshed staad vaishnavee tathaa
(NETHER REGIONS-FLOOR)

एवं दश दिशो रक्षेच्चामुण्डा शववाहना

evam dash disho rakshed chaamundaa shava vaahanaa
(THE 10 DIRECTIONS)

Scatter the remaining seeds around you.

Guru Pooja

Guru, (Master/ Teacher), is the most important entity in our life. He imparts knowledge, which differentiates between animals and us human beings. His blessings are sought before any act. This enables us to align our deeds on knowledge-base, rather than based on whims and impulses.

Those of you who have a guru may meditate on him. Those of you who don't have a guru may meditate on Light streaming upon you as the grace of Divine Guru.

Take some rice and flowers in your hands and say:

|| गुरुर्ब्रह्मा गुरुविष्णुः गुरुर्देवो महेश्वरः ।
गुरुः साक्षात् परंब्रह्म तस्मै श्री गुरवै नमः ॥ ||

Om Gurur Brahmaa gurur vish nuh
Gurur devo mahesh varah
Guru reva param brahma
Tasmai shree guruve namah

Place the rice and flowers in the pooja-plate, and fold your hands.

Guru is Brahma (the Creator, as he creates a new human being out of us, by means of imparting knowledge to us of the Real and the Unreal, and revealing to us the true purpose of our lives), Guru is Vishnu (the Sustainer, as he sustains our existence on this planet by navigating us on our true path), Guru is Maheshwara (Shankara, the Destroyer, as he destroys all ignorance, so that creation/ revelation of knowledge occurs), Guru alone is the Absolute Brahman (the Highest Truth, as he leads us to the realisation of our oneness with God). I bow down to such Guru.

Aadi Pooja (The Beginning)

Pavitrikaranam

Purity is Divinity. Purity of thoughts, words and action precede any sacred act, like worship. Meditate upon a gentle shower of rain drops infusing a sense of joy and optimism in you (taking away the impurity of gloom and distress). Meditate on the rain shower washing the environment around you- the flowers and leaves, the trees and the land, every blade of grass getting bathed in purity.

Take a spoon of water and pour it in the cup of your right palm. Cover it with your left palm. Say :

ॐ अपवित्रः पवित्रो वा सर्वावस्थां गतोऽपि वा।
यः स्मरेत् पुण्डरीकाक्षं स वाह्याभ्यन्तरः शुचिः॥

om apavi trah pavitro vaa sarvaa vas thaam gatopi vaa
yah smareta pundari kaak sham sa
vaahya abhayaan tarah shu chih

Sprinkle the water on yourself and around you.

May the water purify wherever it reaches.

I meditate on the Lotus Eyed, Bhagwaan Vishnu, Whose grace purifies me, both externally and internally, physically, mentally, emotionally and spiritually. Like the lotus is ever pure, even though born out of, and rooted in the mud; like the leaves of the lotus are never wet, even though they are always in water, so also, with a purity of vision and perception, I see only purity around, and become pure (Lotus-Eyed)

Aasan shuddhi

The seat upon which we sit down has to be firm and comfortable (sthiram sukham aasanam- yoga sutra, in reference to our posture- physical, emotional, mental and spiritual.) The seat upon which our consciousness rests, in as much as the seat on which our body rests, should be pure, firm and pleasant. Aasana, at deeper levels also stands for our core values upon which we firmly build our lives.

Seeking purification of our being, as well as our worship seat, take a pinch of rice and petals, put it under your worship seat. Then take kusha, and put this also under your worship seat. Touch the seat with your right hands and say:

ॐ पृथ्वी त्वाया धृता लोका देवित्वं विष्णुना धृता।
त्वं च धारय मां देवि पवित्रं कुरू चासनम् ॥

Om prithvi twayaa dhritaa lokaah devi
twam vishnu naa dhritaa
Twam cha dhaaraya maam devi pavitram kuru cha aasanam

Oh Mother Earth! You uphold all Life! Goddess, You also uphold Lord Vishnu (and, thus all creation). Please hold me too (in your lap), and may You purify my worship seat.

Aachmanan

Water is life. Most of our bodies, 96% or more, is essentially water. In the Gita, Bhagwaan Krishna says, "Of water, I am the sapidity, (rasoham apsu)".

Meditating upon the sacredness and purifying energy of water, take a spoon full of water with your left hand and pour into your right palm, folded as a cup. Say the mantra and sip the water. Again take water, say the next mantra and sip first.

ॐ केशवाय नमः

om kesha vaaya namah (sip the water)

I bow to Keshava, the One Who Rests in Water, Who is the Giver of Water of Life to all beings

ॐ नारायणाय नमः

om naaraa yanaaya namah (sip the water)

I bow to Naaraayana, the Field of Knowledge, from Whom we derive all that we know

ॐ माधवाय नमः

om maadha vaaya namah (sip the water)

I bow to Maadhava, the Sweetness of Bliss, Who grants everlasting peace and happiness.

Now, take water again in your right palm, say the mantra below, and drop the water on your left side, as if washing your hand.

ॐ हृषीकेषाय नमः

om hrishi keshaaya namah

(drop water on your left, as if washing your hand)

I bow to Hrishikesha, the Lord of Senses, Who grants sensual pleasure, and restrain thereof.

Chandan Tilak Dhaaranam (Tikka)

Tilak is a mark put on the forehead, just above the point where the eyebrows meet. About 5 cms inside from that point lies the pitutary gland, also called the Master Gland. The Pitutary gland controls all vital bodily functions. It is also considered as the seat of the Soul- our consciousness, in fact our very being. The Aagyaa chakra is also located in this region, as is the mystical "Third Eye of Wisdom and Intuition".

Meditating on the Third Eye, take sandal paste with the tip of your right-hand's ring-finger, and put the same on your forehead. Say:

|| चन्दनस्य महत्पुण्यं पवित्रं पापनाशनम्।
आपदं हरते नित्यं लक्ष्मी तिष्ठतु सर्वदा॥ ||

chanda nasya mahat punyam pavitram paap naash nam
aapa daam haratey nityam lakshmee vasati sarvadaa

Sandalwood has great merits. It purifies, and destroys all evils. It always takes away troubles, and Goddess Lakshmee ever dwells with it.

Sandalwood gives fragrance and coolness. It is believed that even ordinary trees around a sandal tree become similarly fragrant. Venomous snakes coil around the sandal tree trunk, and lie intoxicated. The fragrance of positive values, attitude and behaviour can intoxicate any one who comes in our circle of influence, and can turn animosity into amiability. As such, all wealth dwells with such a person.

Swasti vaachanam (Offerings of Good Wishes for the Universe)(optional)

ॐ स्वस्ति न इन्द्रो वृद्धश्रवाः स्वस्ति नः पूषा विश्ववेदाः।
स्वस्ति नस्तार्क्ष्यो अरिष्टनेमिः स्वस्ति नो बृहस्पतिर्दधातु॥

ॐ अग्निर्देवता वातो देवता सूर्यो देवता चन्द्रमा
देवता वसवो देवता रुद्रा देवतादित्या
देवता मरुतो देवता विश्वेदेवा देवता
बृहुस्पतिर्देवतेन्द्रो देवता वरुणो देवता।

ॐ द्यौः शन्तिरन्तरिक्षꣳशान्तिः पृथिवी शान्तिरापः
शन्तिरोषधयःशान्तिर्वनस्पतयः
शान्ति विश्वे देवा शान्तिर्ब्रह्म शान्तिः
सर्वꣳशान्तिः शान्तिरेव शान्तिः
सामाशान्ति रेधि॥ सुशान्तिर्भवतु॥
ॐ शान्तिः शान्तिः शान्तिः॥

om swasti na indro bridha shravaha
swasti nah pooshaa vishwa vedaahaa
swasti nastaa rakshyo arishta nemihi
swasti no brihas patir dadhaatu

om agnir devataa vaato devataa sooryo
devataa chandra maa devataa
vasavo devataa rudraa devataa aadityaa
devataa maruto devataa
vishwey deva devataa brihaspa tir devater endro
devata varuno devata

om dhyoho shaantir antariksha gwang
shaan tihi prithivi shaanti raapah
shaantir oushadha yah shantir vanas patayah
shanti vishwey devaa
shaantir brahma shaantihi sarva gwang shaantihi

shaantir eva shaantihi
saamaa shaanti redhi sushaantir bhavatu

om shaantihi om shaantihi om shaantihi

May Indra, the Grand Old One, grant peace! May the animals be peaceful, may the constellation of stars be peaceful, and radiate positive energy for us and destroying all obstacles! May Jupiter, the Enormous One, grant peace by imparting the awareness of enormity of individual self, that each tiny individual is in fact an integral part of one enormity called Conciousness!

May Agni Devata (Fire Energy), Vaayu Devata (Wind Energy), Soorya Devata (Solar Energy), Chandramaa Devata (Lunar Energy), Vasva Devata (Geo-Earth Energy), Rudra Devata (Fierce Transformation Energy), Aaditya Devata (Light Energy), Maruta Devata (Dynamic Swiftness Energy), Vishwa Deva Devata (Universal Control Energy), Brihaspatee Devata (Expansive Energy), Indra Devata (Cognitive-Sensual Energy), Varuna Devata (Water Energy), may operate in harmony and grant peace!!

May the Sky be peaceful, the Space and beyond be peaceful, the Earth and the Waters therein be peaceful, the Herbs (and healing plants) be peaceful, the Plant Kingdom be peaceful, may the Energies that govern the universe be peaceful, may Brahma, the Creator and the Creative Enrgy be peaceful, may all we know and all beyond our knowledge be peaceful. May peace, and peace alone prevail, as a divine melody.

Peace! Peace!! Peace!!!

(Peace signifies a deep state of harmony and propriety, with an absence of any stain of conflict. Peace denotes the natural state of being, which is effortless and without strain. It is reflected in the effortless rise of a blade of grass through the earth, or the movement of earth on its axis as a child's toy-top spinning. Peace is our true nature, and includes a sense of effortless bliss and completeness in the present moment. It is not a goal to be aspired for, but a natural state to be realised.)

Sarvadeva Namaskaaram (Offering of Obesience to Main Dieties)

Mix rice, roli, petals and little water. Take a small pinch of this mixture and sprinkle in the pooja-plate at the end of each mantra. Then take another pinch of the mixture and sprinkle at the end of the next mantra. Meditating on the respective deities as mentioned in the brackets respectively, take a pinch of the mixture and say:

ॐ श्रीमन्महागणाधिपतये नमः।

om shree man mahaa ganaadhi pataye namah
(I bow to Lord Ganesha)

ॐ लक्ष्मीनारायणाभ्यां नमः।

om laxmi naaraa yanaa bhyaam namah
(I bow to Lakshmee- Vishnu)

ॐ उमामहेश्वराभ्यां नमः।

om umaa mahesh waraa bhyaam namah
(I bow to Paarvati- Shiva)

ॐ वाणीहिरण्यगर्भाभ्यां नमः।

om vaanee hiranya garbhaa bhyaam namah
(I bow to Saraswati- Brahma)

ॐ शचीपुरन्दराभ्यां नमः।

om shachi puran daraa bhyaam namah
(I bow to Shachi-Indra)

ॐ मातृपितृ चरणकमलेभ्यो नमः।

om maatri pitri charan kamalebhyo namah
(I bow to the lotus feet of my parents)

ॐ इष्टदेवताभ्यो नमः।

om ishta devetaa bhyo namah
(I bow to my personal deity)

ॐ ग्राम देवताभ्यो नमः।

om graam devetaa bhyo namah
(I bow to the deity of this city)

ॐ वास्तु देवताभ्यो नमः

om vaastu devetaa bhyo namah
(I bow to Vaastu Devataa)

ॐ सर्वेभ्यो देवेभ्यो नमः।

om sarvey bhyo devey bhyo namah

(I bow to all deities)

ॐ सर्वेभ्यो ब्राह्मणेभ्यो नमः।

om sarvey bhyo braah maney bhyo namah
(I bow to all the learned men)

ॐ सिद्धि बुद्धिसहिताय श्रीमन्महागणाधिपतये नमः।

om sidhdhi budhdha sahitaaye
shree man mahaa ganaadhi pataye namah
(I bow to Lord Ganesha, accompanied by Siddhi (Accomplishments), and Buddhi (Intellect).

6. Sankalpa (defination of objective of the pooja) (optional)

Meditate on the worship you are just going to begin, and the blessings you seek.

Take rice, and flower petals in your right hand and say:

ॐ विष्णवे नमः, ॐ विष्णोव नमः विष्णवे नमः।
ॐ अद्य ब्र्ह्मणोऽह्नि द्वितीयपरार्धे
श्री श्वेतवाराहकल्पे वैवस्वत मन्वन्तरेऽष्टाविंशतितमे
कलियुगे कलिप्रथमचरणे भूर्लोके बौद्धावतार
सप्तद्वीपान्तर गते (अमुक...) देशे, (अमुक...) नगरे,
कार्तिक मासे कृष्णे पक्षे आमावस्याम् तिथौ
दीपावली पुण्य पर्वानि (अमुक...) गोत्र समुत्पन्नः
(अमुक...) नामोहम् अद्य शुभवेलायाम् सर्व दोष
निवारण पूर्वकम् भगवती महा लक्ष्मी अनुकम्पा
प्रतिकामः गणेशाम्बिका पूजनम् ततः
च महालक्ष्मी पूजनम् अहम् करिष्ये॥

om vishnavey namah, om vishnavey namah,
om vishnavey namah

om adhya brahmano anhi dwiteeya aparaar dhey
shree shweta vaaraaah kalpey,
saptamey vaivaswat manava antarey
ashtaavinshati tamey kali yugey
kali prathama charaney, bhoor lokey
bauddha avataarey
sapta dweepaantar gatey amreekaa deshey
(or canadaa deshey or england deshey or
bhaarat deshey as the country may be)
houston nagarey
(or chicago nagarey/ london nagarey/
dilli nagarey etc as the city may be)

kaartika maasey, krishney pakshey, aamaavasyaam tithau
deepaa wali punya parvaani kashyap gotrey samutpannaha
(or kaushal gotrey or vatsya gotrey as the case may be. For those
who do not know their gotra, they can say kashyap gotrey)

(amuk) naamko aham
(say your name instead of amuk, for eg, Tarun naamko aham, or
Divya naamko aham)

adhya shubha velaayaam sarva dosha nivaaran poorva kam
bhagwati mahaa lakshmee anu kampaa prati kaamah
ganesh ambikaa poojanam tatah cha
mahaa lakshmee poojanam
aham karishye.

Keep the rice and petals in the poojaa-plate

I bow to Bhagwaan Vishnu.

Today, in the afternoon of the day of Lord Brahma, in the epoch of the White Bear, in the period of the 7th Manu, in the first phase of the age of Kali (Kaliyuga), in the world inhabited on planet Earth, when the Lord has last incarnated as the Buddha, located amongst the seven major islands (continents), in America as country, Houston as the city, in the month of kaartika (named after the constellation krittikaa, or Pleiades), krishna paksha (when moon is waning), on amaavasya, the day of new moon, on the auspicious occasion of deepaawali, I, born in kashyapa gotra, named tarun or divya, today in an auspicious time, having removed all faults therein to the best of my knowledge, desirous of gaining the blessings of Goddess Mahaa Lakshmee , I am performing ritual worship (poojaa) of Lord Ganesha, Maa Paarvati and Goddess Mahaa Lakshmee.

Shree Ganesh-Lakshmi Pooja

Take a pinch of rice and a few petals of flowers in your hands and meditate on Shree Ganeshji, saying:

गजाननं भूतगणादिसेवितं।
कपित्थजम्बुफलचारुभक्षणम्॥
उमासुतं शोकविनाशकारकम्।
नमामि विघ्नेश्वरपादपंकजम्॥

om gajaa nanan bhoota ganaadi sevi tam
kapitha jamboo phala chaaru bhaksha num

umaa sutam shoka vinaash kaara kam
namaami vigh nesh wara paada panka jam

Who has an elephant's face, who is served by all the celestial beings, who eats the fruits of kapitha and jaamun (fruits of our negative karmas, which otherwise can stain our lives with bitter and painful experiences), who is the son of Maa Paarvati (born out of, hence in essence like a mountain in strength and protection), and who destroys all grief, I bow down to the lotus-like feet of the Destroyer of all Obstacles.

Now, meditate on Shree Gauriji, saying:

नमो देव्यै महादेव्यै शिवायै सततं नमः।
नमः प्रकृत्यै भद्रायै नियताः प्रणताः स्म ताम्॥

namo devyei mahaa devyei shivaayei shata tam namah
namah prakrityei bhadraayei niya taah prana taah sma taam

I bow down to the Goddess, the Great Goddess! A hundred bows to the consort of Shiva! I bow to Goddess who is the Primordial Nature, the Auspicious One, the Eternal, and the Essence of Life!

ॐ श्री गणेशाम्बिकाभ्याम् नमः।

om shree ganesha ambikaa bhyam namah

I bow to Lord Ganesh and Maa Paarvati!

Place the rice and petals on the supaari (betel nut)

Ganesha avaahanam:

Again take rice and petals and say:

ॐ गणानां त्वा गणपतिश्श्वामहे
प्रियाणां त्वा प्रियपतिश्श्हवामहे
निधीनां त्वा निधिपातिश्श्हवामहे
वसो मम आहमजानि
गर्भधमात्वमजासि गर्भधम्।

om ganaana twa ganapati gwang hawaa mahey
priyaa naan twa priya pati gwang hawaa mahey
nidhi naan twa nidhi pati gwang hawaa mahey
vaso mam aaham jaani garbha dhammaa
twam jaasi garbha dham

ॐ भूर्भुवः स्वः सिद्धिबुद्धिसहिताय गणपतये नमः
गणपतिमावाह्यामि स्थापयामि पूजयामि च।

om bhur bhuwah swah sidhdhi budhdhi
sahitaaya ganpataye namah
gana patim aavaa hayaami sthaa payaami pooja yaami cha

Place rice and petals on supaari (betel nut).

I offer sacrifices unto the Lord of all celestial beings, the Lord of all that is pleasant, the Lord of all wealth! I bow to Him who dwells as the creative energy in the womb of the Mother Earth (earth element, the grossest differentiation of conscious energy) from which all tangible existence is born.

The one who is immanent in all the three levels of universal creation as creation and creative intelligence, who is the Lord of all celestial beings, I invoke Him, seat Him, and worship Him!

Gauri avaahanam:

Take rice and petals and say:

|| हेमाद्रितनयां देवीं वरदां शङ्करप्रियाम्।
लम्बोदरस्य जननीं गौरीमावाह्याम्यहम्॥ ||

hey maadri tanayam deveem vardaam shankara priyaam
lambo darasya jana neem gauri aavaa hayaam aham

|| ॐ भूर्भुवः स्वः गौर्यै नमः
गौरीमावाह्यामि स्थापयामि पूजयामि च। ||

Om bhur bhuvah swah gauryey namah
aavaaha yaami sthaapa yaami pooja yaami cha

Place the rice and petals on the supaari

Oh daughter of the snow capped Himalayas! Oh Goddess, who are the Beloved of Lord Shankara, bless us! Oh Mother of the Large-Bellied Ganesha, Oh Gauri! I invoke Your benign and motherly presence!

I bow down to Gauri, the Life Force immanent in all the three levels of creation!

I invoke You, seat You, and worship You !

Kalash Pooja (The Divine Container)

Take a pinch of rice and a few petals of flowers in your hands and meditate on the Kalasha as the Space that contains all Creation, and the deities that dwell there in. Seeking their presence during worship, say:

ॐ तत्वा जामि ब्रह्मणा बंधमानस्तदा सास्ते यज्मानो हविर्भिः
अहेड मानोवरुरे हवोद्युरषश्वसमानायुः प्रमोखीः ॥

om tatwaa jaami brahmanaa bandha manas tada
saastey jaj maano haavir bhihi aheda maano varure havo dhyu rasha gwang
samaan ayuhu pramo khihi

कलशस्य मुखे विष्णुः कण्ठे रुद्रः समाश्रितः ।
मूले त्वस्य स्थितो ब्रह्मा मध्ये मातृगणा स्मृताः ॥
कुक्षौ तु सागराः सर्वे सप्तद्वीपा वसुन्धराः ।
ऋग्वेदोऽथ यजुर्वेद सामवेदो ह्यथर्वणः ॥
अङ्गैश्च सहिताः सर्वे कलशं तु समाश्रिताः ।
अत्र गायत्री सावित्री शान्तिः पुष्टिकरी तथा ॥

kalashsya mukhey vish nuhu kanthey rudraha samaa shri taaha
mooley twasya sthito brahma madhye maatri ganah smri taaha
kuk show tu saaga raaha sarvey sapta dwee paa vasun dharaah
rig vedotha yazur vedaha saam vedo hyath varnaha
angeysh cha sahitah sarvey kalasham tu samaa shri taaha
atra gaaya tree saavi tree cha shaan tihi pushti karee tathaa

आयान्तु देवपूजार्थं दुरितक्षकारकाः।
गङ्गे च यमुने चैव गोदावरी सरस्वति॥
नर्मदे सिन्धुकावेरी जलेऽस्मिन् सांनिधिं कुरु।
सर्वे समुद्राः सरितस्तीर्थानि जलदा नदाः॥
आयान्तु मम शान्त्यर्थं दुरितक्षयकारकाः।

aayaantu deva poojaa artham durita akshay kaara kaaha
gangey cha yamuney chaiva godaa varee sarasvati
narmadey sindhu kaaveyree jaley asmin saanni dhim kuru
sarvey samu draaha saritas teer thaani jaladaa nadaah
aayaantu mama shaantya artham durita akshaya kaara kaaha

ॐ आपाम्पतये वरुणाय नमः।
सर्वेभ्यो कलशस्थ देवताभ्यो नमः॥
सर्वेभ्यो कलशस्थ तीर्थेभ्यो नमः।
आवाह्यामि स्थापयामि

om aapaam pataye varu naaye namah
sarvey bhyo kalash astha devtaa bhyo namah
sarvey bhyo kalash asha teerthey bhyo namah
aavaa hyaami sthaa payaami

Place the rice and petals on the Kalasha

May all the Elements dwell in Their most subtle form in the Kalasha, and bless me with the nectar of Life!

May Vishnu dwell in the region of the mouth of the Kalasha, Rudra in the throat; at the base may Brahma dwell, and in the space in between, may all the Mothers (creative energy) dwell; near the sides (waist) may all the Seas, and the seven Islands of that make the world reside in the remaining parts of the body of the Kalasha; Here, may Gayatri, and Savitri, the two primordial energies, grant peace and nourishment to all the Celestial Beings who have been invoked, and who are present during this worship!

May the holy rivers, Ganga,Yamuna, Godavari, Saraswati, Narmada, Indus, and Kaveri, fill the Kalasha with their wealths! May all the Seas, the Rivers, and the Streams come here to grant me peace, and take away all my hardships!

I bow to the Lord of Waters, Varuna. I bow to all the deities who dwell in the Kalasha. I bow to all the holy rivers that dwell in the Kaḷasha. I invoke You all, and offer You seat!

Shodash matrika poojanam

There are 16 creative deities in the Vedic liturgy. They are responsible for the process of creation through progressive differentiation of elements and energies.

Meditating on the 16 –Mothers or creative deities, take rice, petals, and fruit (coconut, if available) in your hands. Seeking their presence during worship, say:

ॐ गणेश साहित गौर्यादि षोडष्मात्रिकाभ्यो नमः ।

om ganesha sahita gaur yaadi shodasha maatri kaa bhyo namah

गौरी पद्मा शची मेधा सावित्री विजया जया।
देवसेना स्वधा स्वाहा मातरो लोकमातरः॥
धृतिः पुष्टिस्तथा तुष्टिरात्मनः कुलदेवता।
गणेशेनाधिका ह्येता वृद्धो पूज्याश्च षोडश॥

gauri padmaa shachi medhaa
saavi tree vijayaa jayaa
deva senaa swadhaa swaahaa
maataro loka maatarah
dhritihi pushtis tatha tushtir
aatmanah kula devataa
ganeshey naadhikaa hyetaa
vridhdho poojyaasha cha shodasha

षोडष्मात्रिकाये नमः
ध्यान आवाह्नम् समर्पयामि।

shodash maatri kaaye namah dhyaan aavaa hanam samar payaami

Place rice and petals on the supaari (betel-nut) in the pooja- plate.

I bow to Lord Ganesha, Maa Gauri, and other 16- Cosmic Mothers

Gauri-Ganesh, Padmaa, Shachi, Medhaa, Savitree, Vijayaa, Jayaa, Devasenaa, Swadhaa, Swaahaa, Maatarah, Lokmaatarah, Dhritihi, Pushtihi, Tushtihi, and Kuladevata may all the 16-Cosmic Mothers be worshipped by me!

I bow to the 16-Cosmic Mothers! I offer meditative invocation unto You all!

Navagraha Devata dhyaan avaahanam

There is an intricate inter-dependence and control between us as individuals (microcosm) and the universe (macrocosm). The movement of the Sun controls our external environment, causing day and night, seasons to change, and life itself to be sustained. The Moon controls our internal environment, our minds, our moods, our response to the external environment apart from our psychosomatic health. Other planets too influence our lives at subtle levels. These planets reflect energy waves upon us, from distant constellations. Our energies are deeply inter woven with that of the universe, much more than we are consciously aware of. Scientific research is progressively taking our knowledge of such matrix to newer frontiers.

Meditating on the 9 planets-deities, take rice and petals in your hands. Seeking their presence during worship, say:

|| ॐ ब्रह्मा मुरारिस्त्रिपुरान्तकारी भानुः शशी भूमिसुतो बुधश्च।
गुरुश्च शुक्रः शनिराहुकेतवः सर्वे ग्रहाः शान्तिकरा भवन्तु॥ ||

om brahmaa muraari tripu raanta kaaree
bhaa nuhu shashee bhoomi suto budhash cha
gurush cha shukrah shani raahu ketawah
sarvey grahaah shaanti karaa bhavantu

सर्वेभ्यो सूर्यादि नवग्रहा देवताभ्यो नमः।
ध्यान् आवाहनम् समर्पयामि।।

sarvey bhyo sooryaa di nava grahaa devataa bhyo namah
dhyaan avaa hanam samar payaami

Place rice and petals on the supaari (betel-nut) in the pooja- plate.

I bow to Brahma, Vishnu and Shankara. They the Triad called GOD- Generation (Creation), Operation(Sustenance) and Destruction (Change). I bow to the Sun, the Moon, the Son of Earth (Mars), Mercury (the Giver of Intellect), Jupiter (the Master-Teacher), Venus (the Illumined, and the Illuminator), Saturn (the Slow paced Giver of Results), Rahu (the Dragon's Head) and Ketu (the Dragon's Tail). May all planet-deities be appeased and bless me with peace.

I bow to the Sun and all the planet-deities. I offer meditative invocation to You all!

Shankha- Ghanta Poojanam (Conch Shell-Poojaa Bell)

Shankha or Conch Shell was blown as a victory sound in battles or upon start or completion of an important task like worship or yagya. Ghanta or the Metal-Plate gong too used to be hit to create a deep metallic sound on similar occasions. Even to this day shankh and ghanta are used to create sound on auspicious occasions. Sound is a primordial energy. It is considered to be more basic than light. The "Big Bang Theory" postulates the release of enormous energy in the form of sound at the beginning of the creation. The Bible too mentions "In the beginning there was Word (sound)."

Meditating on the Sound energy emanating from the conch shell and gong, take rice and petals in your hands. Seeking the presence of the deities that dwell there in during worship, offer meditative invocation, and say:

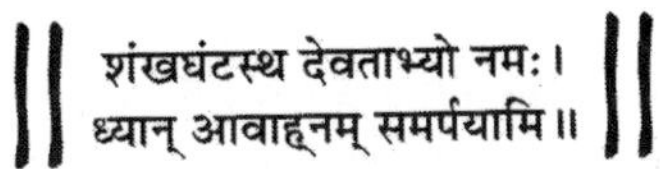
शंखघंटस्थ देवताभ्यो नमः ।
ध्यान् आवाह्नम् समर्पयामि ॥

shankh gantastha devata bhyo namah
dhyaan avaa hanam samar payaami

Place rice and petals on the supaari (betel-nut) in the pooja- plate.

Shree Vidya Maa MahalaxmiPooja (on the Shree yantra)

Maa Maha Lakshmee is the presiding deity of Deepaawali Poojaa. She is also known as Shree

Vidyaa, Shree Tripura Sundari, or simply Shree. This is also a title prefixed before every male name in

India. For married women, Shreemati is prefixed to their names. Shree stands for wealth-material and spiritual. Shree Vidya Maa Mahaa Lakshmee is the bestower of all wealth. She is the primordial Cosmic Mother, the Creatrix. It is with Her spur that Shiva, so far just a "shava" (corpse; Pure Pontential), becomes Shiva. Together they unfold the entire Cosmic creation.

Dhyanam

Meditating on the Mother Maa Maha Lakshmee take a pinch of rice and petals in your hands. Seeking Her presence during worship, say:

या सापद्मासनस्था विपुलकटितटी पद्मपत्रायताक्षी
गम्भीरावर्तनाभिस्तनभरनमिता शुभ्रवस्त्रोत्तरीया।
या लक्ष्मीर्दिव्यरूपैर्मणिगणखचितैः स्नापिता हेमकुम्भैः
सा नित्यं पद्महस्ता मम वसतु गृहे सर्वमाङ्गल्ययुक्ता॥

yaa saa padmaa sanasthaa
vipul kati tatee padma paa traya taak shee
gam bheeraa varta
naabhi stan bhara namitaa
shubhra vastrot tareeyaa
laxmeer divyer gajen drair
mani gana khachi taih snaapitaa
hem kumbhaih nityam saa
padma hastaa vasatu mama
grihey sarva maangalya yuktaa

ॐ महालक्ष्म्यै नमः ।
ध्यान आवाहनम् समर्पयामि ॥

om mahaa lakshmyai namaha
dhyaanam samar payami

Who dwells on the lotus, (a flower that transcends the immediate negative surroundings of mud and water), whose waist is full and beautiful, (indicating the completeness of Her womb, Her creative energy), whose eyes are shaped like a petal of the lotus flower, (Her power of Omniscience), whose navel is round and deep, (Her power to hold the universe with the umbilical chord, through which She infuses Her energy), who is gently bent due to the weight of her breasts, (with which She nourishes all Her children-creation), who is clothed in pure and shinning clothes, (clothes of Truth and Knowledge), who is Lakshmee, (who is goal and its fulfillment), having assumed a divine form, (who is otherwise formless, but assumes a form to enable grasp by cognitive intellect), who is bathed by the King of Divine Elephants with golden vessels adorned with many gems and jewels, (who rejoices and accepts all offerings of devotion), who holds a lotus flower in Her hand, (who grants abundance and a transcendental life symbolised by the lotus flower), may She ever dwell in my home, accompanied with all auspicious energies.

हिरण्यवर्णां हरिणीं सुवर्णरजतस्रजाम् ।
चन्द्रां हिरण्मयीं लक्ष्मीं जातवेदो मऽआवह ॥
ॐ महालक्ष्म्यै नमः ।
आवाहनम् समर्पयामि ॥

om hiranya varnaam harinim suvarna rajata srajaam
chandraam hiranya mayeem laksh meem jaata vedo ma aa vaha
om mahaa lakshmyai namaha
aavaa hanam samar payami

I invoke Maa Lakshmee, whose form is that of heated gold, who is swift as deer, and who is soothing as the Moon!

I bow to Mahaa Lakshmee! I offer invocation to Her!

Sprinkle rice and petals on the shree yantra in the pooja-plate.

Praan Pratishthaapanam (Offering Life-Force, Praana)

Meditate on the Mother, Maa Maha Lakshmee and all the other deities so far invoked. With the intent of infusing them with life by offering a speck of your own life, take a pinch of rice and petals in your hands, say:

ॐ मनो जूतिर्जुषतामाज्यस्य बृहस्पतिर्यज्ञमिमं तनोत्वरिष्टं
यज्ञथ्ंसमिमं दधातु। विश्वे देवास इह मयन्तामोऽम्प्रतिष्ठ ॥

om mano jootir jooshataa maaj yasya

brihas patir yagya mimam tanotwa rishtam
yagya gwang sa imam dadhaatu
vishwey devaa sa ihah maadayan taamo
om pratishtha

॥ अस्यै प्राणाः प्रतिष्ठन्तु अस्यै प्राणाः क्षरन्तु च।
अस्यै देवत्वमर्चायै मामहेति च कश्चन॥ ॥

asyai praa naah pratish thantu
asyai praa naah ksharantu cha
asyai deva twam archaayey
maama heti cha kash chana

Sprinkle rice and petals on the shree yantra in the pooja-plate.

Now, bring all your fingers of the right hand together so that their tips meet at the top. Place the so joined tips of the right hand fingers on the shree yantra. Mediate on enlivening the Deities present, by offering your Life Energy to them. Say:

॥ ॐ गणेशाम्बिकादि सहितं सर्वेभ्यो आवाहित् प्रतिष्ठित्
देवताभ्यो नमः। ततः प्रधान् देवता महा लक्ष्मी देव्यै नमः॥ ॥
सु प्रतिष्ठा वरदा भवन्तु।

om ganesha ambikaa di sahitam sarve bhyo aavaahit devataa bhyo namah
tatah pradhaan devata mahaa lakshmi devye namah
supratish thaa vardaa bhavantu.

Oh Deities, who are present here upon my invocation !I infuse You with the light of my mind, (which is but the Cosmic Mind, like waves and the sea are one only). I seek Brihaspati to infuse wisdom into You, as a result of my humble offerings! May Your Consciousness and Energy be well settled and established for accepting my humble worship! I infuse Life into You! I offer my Life to flow into You! May You Deities be enlivened for my benefit, and nothing else!

I bow to Lord Ganesha, Maa Paarvati, along with all the invoked deities and the presiding deity Maha Lakshmee. May they all be enlivened, and grant me their grace!

The following is offering of courtsies to the deities invoked.

Aasanam (Offering seat to Dieties)

Take a pinch of rice and petals, say the mantra and sprinkle on the shree yantra in the pooja-plate.

नाना रत्न सभाकीर्नम् नाना वर्णविचित्रताम्
आसनम् कल्पितम् देव प्रीत्यार्थम् प्रतिगृह्ताम्।

naanaa ratna sabhaa keernam naanaa varna vichitra tam
aasanam kalpitam deva preetya artham prati grihya taam

ॐ गणेशाम्बिकादि सहितं सर्वेभ्यो आवाहित् प्रतिष्ठित्
देवताभ्यो नमः। ततः प्रधान् देवता महा लक्ष्मी देव्यै नमः॥

om ganesha ambikaa di sahitam

sarvey bhyo aavaa hit pratish thit devataa bhyo namah
tatah pradhaan devata mahaa lakshmi devye namah

I offer my heart as Your throne and foot stool, Oh Goddess and all Deities invoked! Your seat is adorned with many jewels (of positive emotions and thoughts) that illumine the gathering around, and are of very special and uncommon nature! For the sake of my love for You, please occupy the humble seat I offer!

I bow to Lord Ganesha, Maa Paarvati, along with all the invoked deities and the presiding deity Maha Lakshmee. May they all be enlivened, and grant me their grace!

Paadhyam (Offering water to wash feet)

Take a pinch of rice and petals, say the mantra and sprinkle on the shree yantra in the pooja-plate.

पाद्योः पाद्यम् समर्पयामि।

paad yoho paad yam samar payaami

|| ॐ गणेशाम्बिकादि सहितं सर्वेभ्यो आवाहित् प्रतिष्ठित्
देवताभ्यो नमः। ततः प्रधान् देवता महा लक्ष्मी देव्यै नमः॥ ||

om ganesha ambikaa di sahitam
sarvey bhyo aavaa hit pratish thit devataa bhyo namah
tatah pradhaan devata mahaa lakshmi devye namah

I wash Your lotus feet with the waters of my emotions.

I bow to Lord Ganesha, Maa Paarvati, along with all the invoked deities and the presiding deity Maha Lakshmee.

Arghya (Offering water to wash hands)

Take a spoon full of water, say the mantra and put on the shree yantra in the pooja-plate.

हस्तौः अर्घ्यम् समर्पयामि।

hast yoho arghyam samar payaami

ॐ गणेशाम्बिकादि सहितं सर्वेभ्यो आवाहित् प्रतिष्ठित्
देवताभ्यो नमः। ततः प्रधान् देवता महा लक्ष्मी देव्यै नमः॥

om ganesha ambikaa di sahitam
sarvey bhyo aavaa hit pratish thit devataa bhyo namah
tatah pradhaan devata mahaa lakshmi devye namah

I wash Your divine hands with the waters of my devotion.

I bow to Lord Ganesha, Maa Paarvati, along with all the invoked deities and the presiding deity Maha Lakshmee.

Aachamanam (Offering water to wash mouth)

Take a spoon full of water, say the mantra and put on the shree yantra in the pooja-plate.

मुखे आचमनीयम् जलम् समर्पयामि।

mukhey aach manee yam jalam samar payaami

ॐ गणेशाम्बिकादि सहितं सर्वेभ्यो आवाहित् प्रतिष्ठित्
देवताभ्यो नमः। ततः प्रधान् देवता महा लक्ष्मी देव्यै नमः॥

om ganesha ambikaa di sahitam
sarvey bhyo aavaa hit pratish thit devataa bhyo namah
tatah pradhaan devata mahaa lakshmi devye namah

I wash Your beautiful mouth with waters of my love!

I bow to Lord Ganesha, Maa Paarvati, along with all the invoked deities and the presiding deity Maha Lakshmee.

Snaanam (Offering water to bathe)

Take a spoon full of water, say the mantra and put on the shree yantra in the pooja-plate.

स्नानम् जलम् समर्पयामि।

snaanam jalam samar payaami

ॐ गणेशाम्बिकादि सहितं सर्वेभ्यो आवाहित् प्रतिष्ठित्
देवताभ्यो नमः। ततः प्रधान् देवता महा लक्ष्मी देव्यै नमः॥

om ganesha ambikaa di sahitam
sarvey bhyo aavaa hit pratish thit devataa bhyo namah
tatah pradhaan devata mahaa lakshmi devye namah

I bathe Your celestial body with the waters of my life.

I bow to Lord Ganesha, Maa Paarvati, along with all the invoked deities and the presiding deity Maha Lakshmee.

Panchaamrita snaanam (milk, curd, ghee, honey, sugar)

Milk represents nourishment. Curd stands for change- the only unchanging law of life. It represents transformation, and evolution. Ghee stands for fuel of the fire of life. Honey represents the fruition of labour. It is the extract of the essence of goodness that is present in different flowers. It has healing energy too. Sugar represents sweetness in all thoughts, words and action. Sweetness makes life a pleasant experience.

Take a spoon full of panchamrita, say the mantra and put on the shree yantra in the pooja-plate.

पंचामृत स्नानम् समर्पयामि।

panchaa mrita snaanam samar payaami

ॐ गणेशाम्बिकादि सहितं सर्वेभ्यो आवाहित् प्रतिष्ठित्
देवताभ्यो नमः। ततः प्रधान् देवता महा लक्ष्मी देव्यै नमः॥

om ganesha ambikaa di sahitam
sarvey bhyo aavaa hit pratish thit devataa bhyo namah
tatah pradhaan devata mahaa lakshmi devye namah

I bathe You with the Elixir- grant me immortality (in terms of understanding and legacy of good deeds).

I bow to Lord Ganesha, Maa Paarvati, along with all the invoked deities and the presiding deity Maha Lakshmee.

Shuddhodaka (Offering fresh water bath)

Take a spoon full of water, say the mantra and put on the shree yantra in the pooja-plate.

शुद्धोदक् जल स्नानम् समर्पयामि।

shuddho daka jala snaanam samar payaami

ॐ गणेशाम्बिकादि सहितं सर्वेभ्यो आवाहित् प्रतिष्ठित्
देवताभ्यो नमः। ततः प्रधान् देवता महा लक्ष्मी देव्यै नमः॥

om ganesha ambikaa di sahitam
sarvebhyo aavaa hit pratish thit devataa bhyo namah
tatah pradhaan devata mahaa lakshmi devye namah

I bow to Lord Ganesha, Maa Paarvati, along with all the invoked deities and the presiding deity Maha Lakshmee.

Shree Suktam Abhishek (optional)

(It is a very powerful Rig Vedic hymn to Maa Lakshmee It can be read as your daily worship.)

हिरण्यवर्णां हरिणीं सुवर्णरजतस्रजाम् ।
चन्द्रां हिरण्मयीं लक्ष्मीं जातवेदो मऽआवह ॥१॥

hiranya varnaam harinim suvarna rajata srajaam

chandraam hiranya mayeem lakshmeem jaata vedo ma aa vaha

I invoke Maa Lakshmee, whose form is that of heated gold, who is swift as deer, and who is soothing as the Moon!

तां म आवह जातवेदो लक्ष्मीमनपगामिनीम् ।
यस्यां हिरण्यं विन्देयं गामश्वं पुरुषानहम् ॥२॥

taamma aa vaha jaata vedo lakshmee man pagaa mineem
yas yaam hiran yam vinde yam gaama shwam puru shaan aham

I invoke Maa Lakshmee, and beseech Her that She will never desert me and go away! I seek wealth of gold and gems (material wealth), animals like cows and horses (means of livelihood, nourishment and luxurious and swift transportation), lands (for farming; also "region" in terms of economic and financial domain, business empire, field of work, etc.), and men (associates, colleagues, employees, well- wishers, etc.)

अश्वपूर्वां रथमध्यां हस्तिनादप्रमोदिनीम् ।
श्रियं देवीमुपह्वये श्रीर्मा देवीजुषताम् ॥३॥

ashwa poor vaam ratha madhyaam hasti naad pramo dhineem
shriyam devee mupa havye shreer maa devee joosha taam

I invoke Maa Lakshmee, whose chariot is drawn by powerful and swift horses (chariot of our being, drawn by well trained senses and a powerful mind), who rejoices at the sound of the elephants' trumpet (appreciation and recognition of our success by men around), who illumines all life! May She be compassionate and ever dwell in my home (of my being, my existence)!

|| कां सोस्मितां हिरण्यप्राकारामार्द्रां ज्वलन्तीं तृप्तां तर्पयन्तीम्।
पद्मस्थितां पद्मवर्णां तामिहो पह्वये श्रियम् ॥४॥ ||

kam so smitaam hiranya praa kaaraa maad raam jwalan teem
trip taam tarpa yanteem
padmey sthi taam padma varnaam taami hopa havye shriyam

I invoke Maa Lakshmee, who is unfathomable by words and mind (logical intellect; but who can be realised through grace and intuitive awareness), who is ever smiling (giver of joy and bliss), who is adorned with gold jewelry studded with brilliant gems (of valuable values of living and gems of Truth), who showers cause-less grace upon Her beloved children, who grants boons of accomplishments, who is seated on a lotus (of my heart), and whose lustre is that of the lotus flower (soft and soothing, pleasant)!

|| चन्द्रां प्रभासां यशसा ज्वल्न्तीं श्रियं लोके देवजुष्टामुदाराम्।
तां पद्मिनीमीं शरणं प्रपद्येऽलक्ष्मीर्मे नश्यतां त्वां वृणोमि ॥५॥ ||

chand raam prabhaa saam yasha saa jwalan teem
shriyam lokey deva jushtaa mudaa raam

taam padma neemeem sharana maham pra padye
alakshmeer mey nashya taam twaam vrinomi

I seek refuge in and live by the grace of Maa Lakshmee, who is like the moon light, cool and pleasant, who grants peace, whose form is of brilliant light, who is worshipped in all worlds- human and divine, who is extremely benevolent and grants abundant wealth, who fulfills all desires, who dwells at the centre of the lotus (lotus here refers to the geometrical schema of the universe, represented by the shree yantra, where centre is denoted by a dot), whose lustre is that of the lotus flower, who destroys all poverty!

आदित्यवर्णे तपसोऽधिजातो वनस्पतिस्तव वृक्षोऽथ बिल्वः ।
तस्य फलानि तपसानुदन्तु यांतरा याश्च बाह्या अलक्ष्मीः ॥६ ॥

aaditya varney tapso dhi jaato
vanas patis twa vrik shoth bila vaha
tasya phalaani tapsaa nu dantu
maayaan taraa yaash cha baahyaa alakshmeehi

Oh Goddess! Your form shines like the molten rays of the Sun. You give birth to the bael tree, who gives fruits without flowering (You grant the fruits of my good deeds without long incubation in form of flowers of cause and effect), I offer that bael fruit to You (the fruits of my karma, all success I offer unto You). I am putting in my best and intense efforts (tapasya). Kindly remove "alakshmee", ie. all my inefficiencies, my limitations, all obstacles, illness, poverty and negativity (at all levels- material, physical, mental, emotional, spiritual).

उपैतु मां देवसखः कीर्तिश्च मणिना सह ।
प्रादुर्भूतो सुराष्ट्रेऽस्मिन् कीर्तिमृद्धिं ददातु मे ॥७॥

upeytu maam deva sakhah keertish cha manina saha
praadur bhooto suraash tray smin
keertir mridhdhim dadaatu mey

Oh Maa Lakshmee! May I get the highest fame and much wealth! May the friends of gods Kuber and Mani Bhadra be my friends too! I am born (or live) in this nation. May I receive fame and abundance accordingly! (May I be wealthy and famous where I am).

क्षुत्पिपासामलां ज्येष्ठामलक्ष्मीं नाशयाम्यहम् ।
अभूतिमसमृद्धिं च सर्वां निर्णुद मे गृहात् ॥८॥

kshut pipaasaa malaam jyesh thaam alaksh
meem naa shyaa myaham
abhootim asamri dhdhim cha sarvaa nirnuda mey grihaat

I seek to destroy the elder sister of Lakshmee, called Alakshmee (also known as Daridra, the Poverty or Dhoomaavati, the Smoke), who gives hunger and thirst and other forms of wants. Oh Maa Lakshmee! Kindly banish all forms of lacks and wants and all forms of poverty from my home! (Want is the elder sister of fulfillment. Where is not want, there will be no fulfilment. But once fulfilled, the want vanishes. Want is "Alakshmee". Fulfillment is "Lakshmee". I seek such everlasting and absolute fulfillment of my wants and desires, that I never want anymore, that I am ever fulfilled, abundantly)

गन्धद्वारां दुराधर्षां नित्यपुष्टां करीषिणीम्।
ईश्वरीं सर्वभूतानां तामिहोपह्वये श्रियम्॥९॥

gandha dwaa raam duraa dhar shaam nitya
push taam karee shineem
ishwa reem sarva bhootaa naam taami hopa havye shriyam

I invoke Maa Lakshmee, Who rejoices with offerings of fragrances (earth element; positive deeds), Who can never be vanquished (ever victorious, ever successful), Who ever fulfills the desires of Her children by granting them wealth and material possessions, and Who is the presiding Goddess over all beings (hence source of all power)!

मनसः काममाकूतिं वाचः सत्यमशीमहि।
पशूनां रूपमन्नस्य मयि श्रीः श्रयतां यशः॥१०॥

manasah kaama maa kootim vaachas satya mashee mahi
pashoo naam roopa mannasya mayi shreehi shraya taam yashah

Oh Goddess! May my desires be fulfilled, even as they arise in my mind. May my speech be the Truth , (may what I speak become true, and what I speak is the truth). May I have abundance of wealth and beauty (good health). May these ever increase as a result of my good deeds, selfless charity. May the grandeur of my home, ever increase with Your grace!

कर्दमेन प्रजाभूता मयि सम्भवकर्दम।
श्रियं वासय में कुले मातरं पद्मालिनीम्॥११॥

kardamena prajaa bhootaa mayi sambhava kardama
shriyam vaasaya me kuley maataram padma maalineem

The son of Lakshmee named Kardama (literally, Discipline of the Hand; the procreation of Lakshmee is labour, or diligent effort, which later translates into wealth, fame, health and happiness), had his children who populated the world and are thriving today (only diligent labour blessed with grace of Maa Lakshmee flourishes). May my ancestors, who are children of Kardama, ever keep Maa Lakshmee, Who wears the garland of lotus flowers, in my home!

(Goddess of Wealth, Lakshmee, stays in the homes of only those, who offer hard work, perseverance, high values and ethic-based life as a living worship and ritual to Her. Just an outer show of devotion and empty rituals and chanting cannot achieve Her grace.)

|| आपः सृजन्तु स्निग्धानि चिक्लीत वस मे गृहे।
निच देवीं मातंर श्रियं वासय मे कुले ॥१२॥ ||

aapaha srijantu sniga dhaani chikleeta vasa mey grihey
neecha deveem maataram shriyam vaasaya mey kuley

Oh Deity of Water! Please shower your love timely upon us so that harvest of nourishing grains are produced. (Here rains also denote circumstances conducive for our work/ business to flourish.) Oh Chikleeta, Son of Lakshmee! Stay in my home, and make Your Mother also dwell in my home!

(Chikleeta means the Eternal One! The grace of Lakshmee may be eternal upon me!)

|| आर्द्रां पुष्करिणीं पुष्टिं पिंगलां पद्मालिनीम्।
चन्द्रां हिरण्मयीं लक्ष्मीं जातवेदो म आवह ॥१३॥ ||

aadraam push karineem pushteem pinga
laam padma maalineem
chandraam hiranya mayeem lakshameem jaata vedo ma aa vaha

I invoke Maa Lakshmee, Who is the Most Compassionate One by nature, Who is anointed by the waters flowing out of bejeweled vessels, held in the trunks of the elephants of the Keepers-Deities of the Directions, Who nourishes and sustains all moving and non-moving, living and non-living beings and matter, Whose form is that of molten gold, Who is soothing as the Moon, and Who is adorned with a garland of lotus flowers!

आर्द्रां यः करिणीं यष्टिं सुवर्णां हेममालिनीम्।
सूर्यां हिरण्मयीं लक्ष्मीं जातवेदो म आवह ॥१४॥

aadraam yaha kaari neem yashtim suvar
naam hema maalineem
sooryaam hiranya mayeem lakshmeem jaata vedo ma aa vaha

I invoke Maa Mahaa Lakshmee, Who showers cause-less grace and compassion (ie She blesses, whether I deserve or not, whether I sought Her or not, unconditionaly), Who also punishes the evil, Who illumines all creation, whether manifest or unmanifest, like the Sun, and Who is adorned with gold!

तां म आवह जातवेदो लक्ष्मीमनपगामिनीम्।
यस्यां हिरण्यं प्रभूतं गावो दास्योऽश्वान्विन्देयं पुरुषानहम्॥१५॥

taam aa vaha jaata vedo lakshmeem mana pagaa mineem
yasyaam hiranyam prabhoo tam gaavo daasyo shwa vindeyam
purushaa naham

I invoke Maa Lakshmee! May She ever dwell in my home. With Her grace, may I receive abundance of wealth, gold, jewelry, and gems, cows, horses and servants, men who assist and cooperate with me, progeny and more.

यः शुचिः प्रयतो भूत्वा जुहुयादाज्यमन्वहम्।
सूक्तं पंचदशर्चं च श्रीकामः सततम् जपेत्॥१६॥

yaha shuchihi prayato bhootvaa juhu yaa daajya man vaham
sooktam panch dashar cham cha shree kaamaha sata tam japet

Those Who desire wealth and the grace of Maa Mahaa Lakshmee may daily recite this hymn, or offer fire sacrifice with this hymn, after duly purifying himself-physically, mentally, and emotionally.

Vastram (Offering cloth)

Clothing offers protection. By offering symbolic protection, we seek divine protection.

Take a piece of mauli, 3 inches long, say the mantra and put on the shree yantra in the pooja-plate.

वस्त्रम् समर्पयामि।

vastram samar payaami

ॐ गणेशाम्बिकादि सहितं सर्वेभ्यो आवाहित् प्रतिष्ठित
देवताभ्यो नमः। ततः प्रधान् देवता महा लक्ष्मी देव्यै नमः॥

om ganesha ambikaa di sahitam
sarvey bhyo aavaa hit pratish thit devataa bhyo namah
tatah pradhaan devata mahaa lakshmi devye namah

I bow to Lord Ganesha, Maa Paarvati, along with all the invoked deities and the presiding deity Maha Lakshmee.

Aachamanam (Offering fresh water)

Take a spoon full of water, say the mantra and put on the shree yantra in the pooja-plate.

आचमनीयम् समर्पयामि।

aacha manee yam samar payami

Yagyopaveetam (Offering sacred thread- janeyu/ yagyopaveeta)

The sacred thread stands for responsibility. It is a pair of threads, each of three rounds. The knot itself is made in five rounds. It represents the responsibilities arranged in 3s and 5s. Eg. 3s are the thought, word and action. 5s are the 5 sense organs and 5 organs of action. We bestow our responsibility on the deities by offering the sacred thread.

Take the sacred thread, say the mantra and put on the shree yantra in the pooja-plate

यज्ञोपवीतम् समर्पयामि।

yagyo paveetam samar payaami

ॐ गणेशाम्बिकादि सहितं सर्वेभ्यो आवाहित् प्रतिष्ठित्
देवताभ्यो नमः। ततः प्रधान् देवता महा लक्ष्मी देव्यै नमः॥

om ganesha ambikaa di sahitam
sarvey bhyo aavaa hit pratish thit devataa bhyo namah
tatah pradhaan devata mahaa lakshmi devye namah

I bow to Lord Ganesha, Maa Paarvati, along with all the invoked deities and the presiding deity Maha Lakshmee.

Aachamanam (Offering fresh water)

Take a spoon full of water, say the mantra and put on the shree yantra in the pooja-plate.

आचमनीयम् समर्पयामि।

aacha manee yam samar payami

Upa Vastram (Offering the minor clothing)

Take a piece of mauli, 3 inches long, say the mantra and put on the shree yantra in the pooja-plate.

उपवस्त्रम् समर्पयामि।

upa vastram samar payaami

|| ॐ गणेशाम्बिकादि सहितं सर्वेभ्यो आवाहित् प्रतिष्ठित्
देवताभ्यो नमः। ततः प्रधान् देवता महा लक्ष्मी देव्यै नमः॥ ||

om ganesha ambikaa di sahitam
sarvey bhyo aavaa hit pratish thit devataa bhyo namah
tatah pradhaan devata mahaa lakshmi devye namah

I bow to Lord Ganesha, Maa Paarvati, along with all the invoked deities and the presiding deity Maha Lakshmee.

Chandanam (Offering sandal wood paste)

Take a little chandan paste with a petal, say the mantra and put on the shree yantra in the pooja-plate.

चन्दनम् समर्पयामि ।

chandanam samar payaami

|| ॐ गणेशाम्बिकादि सहितं सर्वेभ्यो आवाहित् प्रतिष्ठित्
देवताभ्यो नमः । ततः प्रधान् देवता महा लक्ष्मी देव्यै नमः ॥ ||

om ganesha ambikaa di sahitam
sarvey bhyo aavaa hit pratishthit devataa bhyo namah
tatah pradhaan devata mahaa lakshmi devye namah

I bow to Lord Ganesha, Maa Paarvati, along with all the invoked deities and the presiding deity Maha Lakshmee.

Akshatam (Offering rice, unbroken pieces)

Rice stands for the water element at the subtle level, transformed into nourishment. Unbroken pieces of rice (akshata) stand for firm resolve, and unbroken promises. While we seek to obtain divine promises of support, we also offer our promise to do our humble bit in life.

Take a pinch of rice, say the mantra and put on the shree yantra in the pooja-plate.

अक्षतान् समर्पयामि।

aksha taan samar payaami

ॐ गणेशाम्बिकादि सहितं सर्वेभ्यो आवाहित् प्रतिष्ठित्
देवताभ्यो नमः। ततः प्रधान् देवता महा लक्ष्मी देव्यै नमः॥

om ganesha ambikaa di sahitam
sarvey bhyo aavaa hit pratish thit devataa bhyo namah
tatah pradhaan devata mahaa lakshmi devye namah

I bow to Lord Ganesha, Maa Paarvati, along with all the invoked deities and the presiding deity Maha Lakshmee.

Pushpam (Offering a flower)

Flower stands for the earth element at the subtle level. It also represents the dynamic process of action, which later leads to fruition. We offer all our actions to the Divine in form of a flower. May our actions be as beautiful, as effortless, as perfect, as fragrant, as tender and as complete as the flower we offer.

Take a flower, say the mantra and put on the shree yantra in the pooja-plate.

पुष्पम् समर्पयामि।

push pam samar payaami

ॐ गणेशाम्बिकादि सहितं सर्वेभ्यो आवाहित् प्रतिष्ठित्
देवताभ्यो नमः। ततः प्रधान् देवता महा लक्ष्मी देव्यै नमः॥

om ganesha ambikaa di sahitam
sarvey bhyo aavaa hit pratish thit devataa bhyo namah
tatah pradhaan devata mahaa lakshmi devye namah

I bow to Lord Ganesha, Maa Paarvati, along with all the invoked deities and the presiding deity Maha Lakshmee.

Doorvaa (Offering blades of grass)

Grass represents fertility and growth. It also represents humility, and utility of the highest order. It stands for ability to withstand adversity. May we learn from the humble blades of grass.

Take a few blades of grass, say the mantra and put on the shree yantra in the pooja-plate.

दुर्वान्कुरान् समर्पयामि।

doorva ankuraan samar payaami

ॐ गणेशाम्बिकादि सहितं सर्वेभ्यो आवाहित् प्रतिष्ठित्
देवताभ्यो नमः। ततः प्रधान् देवता महा लक्ष्मी देव्यै नमः॥

om ganesha ambikaa di sahitam
sarvey bhyo aavaa hit pratish thit devataa bhyo namah
tatah pradhaan devata mahaa lakshmi devye namah

I bow to Lord Ganesha, Maa Paarvati, along with all the invoked deities and the presiding deity Maha Lakshmee.

Sugandhit Dravyam (Offering fragrance-essence of flowers, Itr)

Fragrance represents the earth element. It is the subtlest part of a flower, yet its very identity and fundamental intent. Fragrance travels against the breeze. Hence it represents upholding our core values even in face of trials and adversity.

Pour a little itr (essence of flower, scent)on a petal, say the mantra and put on the shree yantra in the pooja-plate.

सुगन्धित् द्रव्यम् समर्पयामि।

sugan dhit dravyam samar payaami

|| ॐ गणेशाम्बिकादि सहितं सर्वेभ्यो आवाहित् प्रतिष्ठित्
देवताभ्यो नमः। ततः प्रधान् देवता महा लक्ष्मी देव्यै नमः॥ ||

ganesha ambikaa di sahitam
sarvey bhyo aavaa hit pratish thit devataa bhyo namah
tatah pradhaan devata mahaa lakshmi devye namah

I bow to Lord Ganesha, Maa Paarvati, along with all the invoked deities and the presiding deity Maha Lakshmee.

Sindoor (Offering sindoor)

Sindoor is made of mercury and sulphur fused together as mercuric sulphide. Mercury represents the essence of masculine energy which is cool and watery. Sulphur represents the essence of feminine energy, which is hot and fire-like. Sindoor represents the process of becoming one of the two polarities of energy, the yin and the yang, the light and darkness, the pure potential and the dynamic, and such like. Sindoor is therefore worn as a mark of marriage by most Hindu women in the parting of their hair or as a round mark on their forehead. It represents the creative force through unison of energies. We seek the creative force to play in our lives by offering sindoor.

Take a little sindoor on a petal, say the mantra and put on the shree yantra in the pooja-plate.

सिन्दूरम् समर्पयामि।

sindooram samar payaami

|| **ॐ गणेशाम्बिकादि सहितं सर्वेभ्यो आवाहित् प्रतिष्ठित्**
देवताभ्यो नमः। ततः प्रधान् देवता महा लक्ष्मी देव्यै नमः॥ ||

om ganesha ambikaa di sahitam
sarvey bhyo aavaa hit pratish thit devataa bhyo namah
tatah pradhaan devata mahaa lakshmi devye namah

I bow to Lord Ganesha, Maa Paarvati, along with all the invoked deities and the presiding deity Maha Lakshmee.

Naanaa Parimal Dravyam (Offering variety of elements-roli, abir, gulal, haldi)

Take a pinch of each of the above- roli, abir, gulal, haldi (turmeric tuber), karjamba, and lotus seeds. Say the mantra and put on the shree yantra in the pooja-plate, one by one.

नाना परिमल द्रव्यम् समर्पयामि।

naanaa parimal dravyam samar payaami

ॐ गणेशाम्बिकादि सहितं सर्वेभ्यो आवाहित् प्रतिष्ठित्
देवताभ्यो नमः। ततः प्रधान् देवता महा लक्ष्मी देव्यै नमः॥

ganesha ambikaa di sahitam
sarvey bhyo aavaa hit pratish thit devataa bhyo namah
tatah pradhaan devata mahaa lakshmi devye namah

I bow to Lord Ganesha, Maa Paarvati, along with all the invoked deities and the presiding deity Maha Lakshmee.

Dhoopam (Offering Incense)

The smoke emanating from the dhoop and incence represents the air element. Air represents breath. It also represents the vital process of differentiation beginning the space element which differentiates into air, then fire, water and finally earth, the grossest element of creation. Air represents movement and change. It also stands for ultimate flexibility and ability to blend. It assumes the shape of the container it dwells in. May we accept, and be accepted in all situations of life. May we accept changes, and change seem-lessly, when needed to.

With your hands, wave the smoke of the dhoopam towards the pooja-plate, and say the mantra.

धूपम् आघ्रापयामि।

doopam aaghraa payaami

|| ॐ गणेशाम्बिकादि सहितं सर्वेभ्यो आवाहित् प्रतिष्ठित्
देवताभ्यो नमः। ततः प्रधान् देवता महा लक्ष्मी देव्यै नमः॥ ||

ganesha ambikaa di sahitam
sarvey bhyo aavaa hit pratish thit devataa bhyo namah
tatah pradhaan devata mahaa lakshmi devye namah

I bow to Lord Ganesha, Maa Paarvati, along with all the invoked deities and the presiding deity Maha Lakshmee.

Deepam (Offering the Light)

The Flame of light represents the fire element. It sustains praana, the life-force that flows in within us in subtle channels (called naadis). It is replenished through breath. The fire element causes the sense of sight and speech to function, as well as the metabolic function in the human body, which is essential to burn glucose and release its subtle content – energy. Fire also represents the all consuming energy that reduces all things to ashes, releasing the subtle contents into the universe. Fire sacrifice, known as yagya, is integral part of vedic ritual. It is also a part of Jewish tradition of worship. In the Christian and Islamic tradition which follow the Old Testament, God reveals Himself to Moses in form of fire. We offer the fire element, seeking divine warmth and guidance (light) as we traverse our paths on this planet.

With your hands, wave the light of the lamp towards the pooja-plate, and say the mantra.

दीपम् दर्शयामि।

deepam darsha yaami

ॐ गणेशाम्बिकादि सहितं सर्वेभ्यो आवाहित् प्रतिष्ठित्
देवताभ्यो नमः। ततः प्रधान् देवता महा लक्ष्मी देव्यै नमः॥

om ganesha ambikaa di sahitam
sarvey bhyo aavaa hit pratish thit devataa bhyo namah
tatah pradhaan devata mahaa lakshmi devye namah

I bow to Lord Ganesha, Maa Paarvati, along with all the invoked deities and the presiding deity Maha Lakshmee.

Take a spoon full of water, and wash your hands on your left side.

Naivedyam (Offering the fruits)

Food satiates hunger, by nourishing our body and pleasing our senses. The food is consumed by the five primary life forces in our body. They are called praana, apaana, vyaana, samaana, and udaana. We offer food, so that we are abundantly satiated, that we never hunger.

Take pancha mewa(dry fruits) and a piece of sweet, say the mantra and put on the shree yantra in the pooja-plate.

|| नैवेद्यम् निवेद्यामि क्षुधातृप्तिार्थे
नैवेद्यम् समर्पयामि। ||

naivedyam niveda yaami kshudha tripi
arthey naivedyam samar payaami

|| ॐ गणेशाम्बिकादि सहितं सर्वेभ्यो आवाहित् प्रतिष्ठित्
देवताभ्यो नमः। ततः प्रधान् देवता महा लक्ष्मी देव्यै नमः॥ ||

om ganesha ambikaa di sahitam
sarvey bhyo aavaa hit pratish thit devataa bhyo namah
tatah pradhaan devata mahaa lakshmi devye namah

I bow to Lord Ganesha, Maa Paarvati, along with all the invoked deities and the presiding deity Maha Lakshmee.

ॐ प्रणाय स्वाहा।

om praa naya swaa haa

ॐ अपानाय स्वाहा।

om apaa naaya swaa haa

ॐ व्यानाय स्वाहा।

om vyaa naaya swaa haa

ॐ समानाय स्वाहा।

om samaa naaya swaa haa

ॐ उदानाय स्वाहा।

om udaa naaya swaa haa

Jalam (Offering fresh water)

Take a spoon full of water, say the mantra and put on the shree yantra in the pooja-plate.

पुनः हस्तमुखप्रक्षाल्यार्थे
जलम् समर्पयामि।

punah hasta mukha prakshaal yarthey jalam samar payaami

Udwartanam (Offering of cleansing)

Udwartana is also called ubtan in common Hindi. It is used to deeply cleanse the skin. Brides and grooms are applied ubtan as a ritual just before marriage. It signifies cleansing of all deep seated dirt from the past, enabling us to move forward in life with a "clean skin". May we be cleansed from the dark shadows of our past.

Take a little sandalwood paste on a petal, say the mantra and put on the shree yantra in the pooja-plate.

उद्वतनार्थे गंधम् समर्पयामि।

udwarta naarthey gandham samar payaami

ॐ गणेशाम्बिकादि सहितं सर्वेभ्यो आवाहित् प्रतिष्ठित्
देवताभ्यो नमः। ततः प्रधान् देवता महा लक्ष्मी देव्यै नमः॥

om ganesha ambikaa di sahitam
sarvey bhyo aavaa hit pratish thit devataa bhyo namah
tatah pradhaan devata mahaa lakshmi devye namah

I bow to Lord Ganesha, Maa Paarvati, along with all the invoked deities and the presiding deity Maha Lakshmee.

Ritu phalam (Offering of seasonal fruit)

Fruits represent the space element. Space contains all. The fruit contains the seeds, which in turn contain not only a tree, but the possibility of infinite number of forests. The fruits of our actions contain infinite possibilities of consequences. We, therefore, offer the fruits of our actions to the Divine Mother. She, in Her supreme compassion and love for us, will allow only beneficial consequences to materialise for us, thus we pray.

Take a seasonal fruit or a banana, say the mantra and put on the shree yantra in the pooja-plate.

ऋतु फलम् समर्पयामि।

ritu phalam samar payaami

ॐ गणेशाम्बिकादि सहितं सर्वेभ्यो आवाहित् प्रतिष्ठित्
देवताभ्यो नमः। ततः प्रधान् देवता महा लक्ष्मी देव्यै नमः॥

om ganesha ambikaa di sahitam
sarvey bhyo aavaa hit pratish thit devataa bhyo namah
tatah pradhaan devata mahaa lakshmi devye namah

I bow to Lord Ganesha, Maa Paarvati, along with all the invoked deities and the presiding deity Maha Lakshmee.

Mukha shuddhi (Mouth Freshner)

At times, what we eat leaves a bad odour and taste in the mouth. A mouth freshner cleanses the breath, and makes it pleasant. The exhaled breath does not disturb others with bad odour. The exhaled breath also represents spoken words. A fresh mouth should speak pleasant words. Lord Jesus Christ said that a man is defiled not so much by what goes into his mouth, but by what comes out of it. Foul breath can be corrected by mouth freshner. Foul words can leave deep, indelible marks. May we become aware of the words that leave our mouth. May our words be as fragrant as the mouth freshner.

Take a clove, cardamom, and betel leaf (paan)

(if available), say the mantra and put on the shree yantra in the pooja-plate.

|| इला लवंगादि साहितम्
ताम्बूल पत्रम् समर्पयामि। ||

elaa lawanga aadi sahitam taambool patram samar payaami

|| ॐ गणेशाम्बिकादि सहितं सर्वेभ्यो आवाहित् प्रतिष्ठित्
देवताभ्यो नमः। ततः प्रधान् देवता महा लक्ष्मी देव्यै नमः॥ ||

om ganesha ambikaa di sahitam
sarvey bhyo aavaa hit pratish thit devataa bhyo namah
tatah pradhaan devata mahaa lakshmi devye namah

I bow to Lord Ganesha, Maa Paarvati, along with all the invoked deities and the presiding deity Maha Lakshmee.

Akhand Shree Phalam (Offering of coconut)

Coconut represents a human head. When skinned of all fibres, spots resembling eyes, nose and mouth can be seen. We offer our ego as a coconut, as an act of complete surrender to the Divine Mother.

Take a coconut, say the mantra and put on the shree yantra in the pooja-plate.

अखण्डश्रीफलम् समर्पयामि।

akhanda shree phalam samar payaami

ॐ गणेशाम्बिकादि सहितं सर्वेभ्यो आवाहित् प्रतिष्ठित्
देवताभ्यो नमः। ततः प्रधान् देवता महा लक्ष्मी देव्यै नमः॥

om ganesha ambikaa di sahitam
sarvey bhyo aavaa hit pratish thit devataa bhyo namah
tatah pradhaan devata mahaa lakshmi devye namah

I bow to Lord Ganesha, Maa Paarvati, along with all the invoked deities and the presiding deity Maha Lakshmee.

Dakshinaa dravyam (Offering of wealth)

A spec of our earning is offered, seeking abundance of wealth

Take a coin (dollar/ cent), say the mantra and put on the shree yantra in the pooja-plate.

दक्षिणा द्रव्यम् समर्पयामि।

dak shinaa dravyam samar payaami

ॐ गणेशाम्बिकादि सहितं सर्वेभ्यो आवाहित् प्रतिष्ठित्
देवताभ्यो नमः। ततः प्रधान् देवता महा लक्ष्मी देव्यै नमः॥

om ganesha ambikaa di sahitam
sarvey bhyo aavaa hit pratish thit devataa bhyo namah
tatah pradhaan devata mahaa lakshmi devye namah

I bow to Lord Ganesha, Maa Paarvati, along with all the invoked deities and the presiding deity Maha Lakshmee.

Anga poojaa

Many Deity-Energy dwell in the divine form of Maa Mahaa Lakshmee. Meditate upon the various deities in the respective parts of Maa's body. Take a pinch of rice and petals, say one mantra, and sprinkle the same on the shree yantra. Again take the same, say the next mantra, and sprinkle on the shree yantra, and so on.

ॐ चपलायै नमः। पादौ पूजयामि।

om chapalaayei namah paadou poojyaami (feet) (The Swift)

ॐ चञ्चलायै नमः। जानुनी पूजयामि।

om chanchalaayei namah
jaanuni poojyaami (knees)
(The Dynamic)

ॐ कमलायै नमः। कटिं पूजयामि।

om kamalaayei namah
katim poojyaami (waist)
(The Lotus-like)

ॐ कात्यायन्यै नमः। नाभिं पूजयामि।

om kaatyaa yanyei namah
naabhim poojyaami (naval)
(The Unmanifest Dimension)

ॐ जगन्मात्रै नमः। जठरं पूजयामि।

om jaganmaatrayei namah
jatharam poojyaami (stomach)
(The Universal Mother)

ॐ विश्ववल्लभायै नमः। वक्षस्थलं पूजयामि।

om vishwa vallabhaayei namah
vaksha sthalam poojyami (breasts)
(The Beloved of the Universe)

ॐ कमलवासिन्यै नमः। हस्तौ पूजयामि।

om kamal vaasinyei namah
hastau poojyaami (hands)
(The Lotus-Dweller)

ॐ पद्माननायै नमः। मुखं पूजयामि।

om padmaa nanaayei namah
mukham poojyaami (mouth)
(The Lotus-Visioned)

ॐ कमलपत्राक्ष्यै नमः। नेत्रत्रयं पूजयामि।

om kamal patrakshayei namah
netra trayam poojyaami (3 eyes)
(The Lotus Petal-Eyed)

ॐ श्रियै नमः। शिरः पूजयामि।

om shriyei namah
shirah poojyaami (head)
(The Wealth)

ॐ महालक्ष्म्यैः नमः। सर्वाङ्गं पूजयामि।

om mahalakshamyei namah
sarvaanga poojyaami (entire body)
(The Great Goal)

Ashta siddhi poojan

There are 8 major accomplishments, which form a part of Maa's grace and entourage. Take a pinch of rice and petals, say one mantra, and sprinkle the same on the shree yantra. Again take the same, say the next mantra, and sprinkle on the shree yantra, and so on. Begin from the top-side middle of the yantra which is considered the east. Move in clockwise direction around periphery of the yantra. In case of doubt, just sprinkle on the yantra. Say:

ॐ अणिम्ने नमः।
om animney namah (east)
(The power to condense)

ॐ महिम्ने नमः।
om mahimney namah (south east)
(The power to expand)

ॐ गरिम्णे नमः।
om garimney namah (south)
(The power to densify)

ॐ लघिम्ने नमः।
om laghimney namah (southwest)
(The power to rarify)

ॐ प्राप्त्यै नमः।
om praaptayei namah (west)
(The power to achieve)

ॐ प्राकाम्यै नमः।
om praakaamyei namah (northwest)
(The power to desire)

ॐ ईशितायै नमः।

om ishitaayei namah (north)
(The power to accomplish)

ॐ वशितायै नमः ।
om vashitaayei namah (northeast)
(The power to impress)

Ashta lakshmi poojan

Maha Lakshmee has 8 primary forms, called Ashta-Lakshmee. Each represents a distinct energy of wealth, without which what we refer to as wealth is meaningless.

Mix rice, roli, petals and little water. Take a small pinch of this mixture and sprinkle on the shree yantra in the pooja-plate at the end of each mantra. Then take another pinch of the mixture and sprinkle at the end of the next mantra. Meditating on the respective deities as mentioned in the mantra respectively, take a pinch of the mixture and say:

ॐ आद्यालक्ष्म्यै नमः ॥१॥

om aadyaa lakshamyee namah
(I bow to the Goddess of Primordial Wealth, the source of all wealth.)

ॐ विद्यालक्ष्म्यै नमः ॥२॥

om vidyaa lakshamyee namah
(I bow to the Goddess of Wealth of Knowledge, which creates and keeps all wealth.)

ॐ सौभाग्यलक्ष्म्यै नमः ॥३ ॥

om sau bhaagya lakshamyee namah
(I bow to the Goddess of Wealth of Good Fortune,
which enables us to strike gold.)

ॐ अमृतलक्ष्म्यै नमः ॥४ ॥

om amrita lakshamyee namah
(I bow to the Goddess of Wealth of Elixir,
that preserves and protects till eternity)

ॐ कामलक्ष्म्यै नमः ॥५ ॥

om kaama lakshamyee namah
(I bow to the Goddess of Wealth of Desire,
which stokes the passion to possess and enjoy.)

ॐ सत्यलक्ष्म्यै नमः ॥६ ॥

om satya lakshamyee namah
I bow to the Goddess of Wealth of Truth,
which leads to self-realisation, our highest human need.)

ॐ भोगलक्ष्म्यै नमः ॥७ ॥

om bhoga lakshamyee namah
(I bow to the Goddess of Wealth of Indulgence,
which enables us to enjoy what we have.)

ॐ योगलक्ष्म्यै नमः ॥८ ॥

om yoga lakshamyee namah
(I bow to the Goddess of Wealth of Yoga,
which unites our consciousness with Divinity.)

Kuber poojan

Meditate on Yaksha Raaja Kuber, the Keeper of Celestial Wealth.

Take a pinch of rice and petals, say the mantra and put on the shree yantra in the pooja-plate.

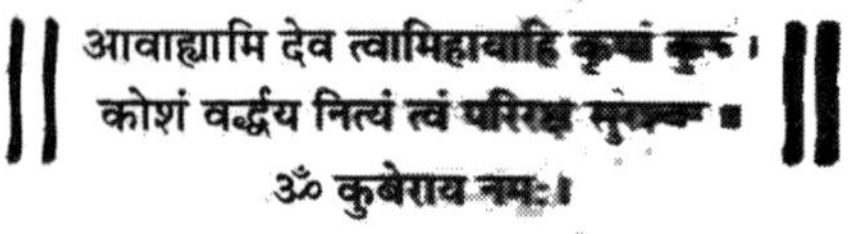
आवाह्यामि देव त्वामिहायाहि कृपां कुरु ।
कोशं वर्द्धय नित्यं त्वं परिरक्ष सुरेश्वर ॥
ॐ कुबेराय नमः ।

aavaa hyaami deva twaa mihaa yaahi kripaam kuru
kosham vardhaya nityam twam pari raksha suresh wara
om kuberaaya namaha

धनदाय नमस्तुभ्यं निधिपद्माधिपाय च।
भगवन् त्वत्प्रसादेन धनधान्यादिसम्पदः ॥

dhana daaya namas tubhyam nidhi padmaa dhi paaya cha
bhagwan twat prasaa dena dhana dhaanyaa di samm padah

I invoke You, Lord, please grace this worship by Your presence

May You ever enhance my treasures of wealth, and protect the same too, Oh Lord of Deities!

I bow to Lord Kubera

I bow to You Lord! You are the Burser (giver) of Wealth, and all the treasures are obtained with your grace alone!

Dawat Pooja (Books of Accounts/ Pen) (optional)

Place the inkpot in front of the altar.Tie the mauli (red thread) around it. Put a tilak on the bottle, and some rice and petals. Say:

ॐ श्री महाकाल्यै नमः ।

om shree maha kaalyei namaha

Now tie mauli around the pen, put a tilak on it, sprinkle some rice and petals on it and say:

कालिके ! त्वं जगन्मातर्मसिरूपेण वर्तते ।
उत्पन्ना त्वं च लोकानां व्यवहारप्रसिद्धये ॥

kaalikey twam jagan maatar masi roopen varta sey
utpanna twam cha lokaa naam vyavhaar prasidhdhye

I bow to Maa Maahaa Kaali!

Oh Kaali! You the Mother of the Universe! May You dwell as ink, so that letters that are born of You, are well received amongst all men I interact with!

Now tie mauli around the pen, put a tilak on it, sprinkle some rice and petals on it and say:

लेखनी निर्मिता पूर्वं ब्रह्मणा परमेष्ठिना ।
लोकांना च हितार्थाय तस्मातां पूजयाम्यहम् ॥

lekhanee nirmitaa poor vam brahmanaa parmesh thinaa
lokaa naam cha hitaar thaaya tas maattaam poojayaa mya ham

ॐ लेखनीस्थायै देव्यै नमः।

om lekhinee sthayee devyaei namaha

शास्त्राणां व्यवहाराणां विद्यानामाप्नुयाद्यतः।
अतस्त्वं पूजयिष्यामि मम हस्ते स्थिरा भव॥

shastraa naam vyava haaraa naam vidyaa
naam aapnu yaa dhyatah
atas twam poojayi shyaami mam hastey sthiraa bhav

Oh Pen! Before you became a pen, you were with Lord Brahmaa in your subtle form. For the benefit of all, I worship you now. I bow to the Goddess who dwells in the pen. For the expression for knowledge and learning, and for the purpose of communication with all, I worship you and request you to remain stable in my hand.

Take the cash book/ dairy/ notebook, and make a swastika on it or just a tilak with roli, or paste of chandan powder and saffron. Meditate on Goddess Saraswati, the Goddess of Learning. Sprinkle rice and petals on it and say:

या कुन्देन्दुतुषारहारधवला या शुभ्रवस्त्रावृता
या वीणावरदण्डमण्डितकरा या श्वेतद्मासना।
या ब्रह्माच्युतशङ्करप्रभृतिभिर्देवैः सदा वन्दिता
सा मां पातु सरस्वती भगवती निःशेषजाड्यापहा॥

yaa kundendu tushaar haar dhawalaa
yaa shubra vastraa vritaa
yaa veenaa vara danda mandit karaa
yaa shweta padmaa sanaa

yaa brahmaa chyut shankara pra bhriti bhir devyeeh
sadaa vanditaa
saa maam paatu saras vatee bhag watee
nih shesha jaadyaa pahaa

ॐ वीणापुस्तकधारिण्यै श्रीसरस्वत्यै नमः।

om veenaa pustaka dhaa rinyee shree saras watyei namaha.

Who wears the garland of the buds of kunda, the flower which is white like the Moon, Who wears Purity as white garment, Whose hands are adorned by Veenaa (a musical instrument), who dwells on white lotus flower, Who is ever worshipped by Brahma, Vishnu and Shankara in form of Supreme Knowledge, May that Goddess Saraswati protect me (protect my learning and protect me from ignorance/ false knowledge)! May She take away my ignorance completely, leaving no trace of it!

I bow to the Maa Saraswatee, Who holds the Veenaa in one hand, and the Book in another!

Veena signifies music, the ease and sweetness of learning, and the application of learning to all spheres of life, making living a beautiful, and transcendental experience. The Book signifies all codified, logical knowledge/ information, which is fundamental to human life. Together, they signify Knowledge, both manifest and unmanifest, which forms the basis know-how of creation.

Show incense and lamp to the ink-pot, the pen and the notebook just now worshipped.

Deepa maalikaa poojan (the lamps)

(In case you have several lamps to be lit, for decorating your house)

Place 3,5,7,9,11, or more earthen lamps in a plate. Fill the same with ghee (clarified butter) Fill one lamp with til(seasme) oil/ mustard oil/ any vegetable oil. Place think cotton wicks in each of the lamps. Light all of them. Say:

ॐ दीपावल्यै नमः।
त्वं ज्योतिस्तवं रविश्चन्द्रो विद्युदग्निश्च तारकाः।
सर्वेषां ज्योतिषां ज्योतिर्दीपावल्यै नमो नमः॥

om deepaa valyei namaha
twam jyotis twam ravish chandro vidhyud agnish cha taar kaah
sarvey shaam jyoti shaam jyotir deepaa valyei namo namah

Place some rice grains, and juicy whole fruit (orange, etc) next to the plate containing lamps. Fold your hands and offer your respect to the lamps, seeking them to light up all darkness, and, illumine and lead you on the right path in life

After the pooja, place these lamps at the main door of your house, or other places around your house as you wish to.

Aarti

Take a small steel plate (copper/ brass/silver would also do). Place a very small bowl in it. Take a piece of camphor and light it with a lamp, then place in the bowl. Or, place the piece of camphor in the bowl and light it with a burning matchstick, lighter, or candle. Hold the plate with your right hand and offer the camphor-flame to dieties by swaying the plate gently in front of the pooja- plate. In case the camphor is about to burn out, put more pieces of camphor into the bowl. Other members of the family/ friends who are present, and wish to perform aarti can do the same with the aarti plate, and say the same mantra as given below. You may stand up, and bend down, if you wish. Say the mantra:

om ida gwang havihi praja nanam mey asto dash veera gwang
sarva gana gwang swas taye aatma sani prajaa sani pashu sani
loka sanya bhaya sanihi agnihi prajaam baho laambey karo
twan nam payo reto asmaa su dhatta

कर्पूरगौरं करुणावतारं संसारसारं भुजगेन्द्रहारम्
सदा वसन्तं हृदयारविन्दे भवं भवानी सहितं नमामि।

karpur gauram karunaa vataaram
sansaar saaram bhuja gendra haaram
sadaa vasan tam hridayaa ravindam
bhavam bhavaani sahitam namaami

Fair as camphor, Maa Paarvati, and compassion incarnate, Shiva, The essence of creation, Maa Paarvati, and adorned with the garland of serpents (Energy), Shiva,

May you ever dwell in the lotus abode of my heart.Oh! Shiva-Paarvati, in form of Bhavam, Pure Potential, and Bhavani, Dynamic Energy! I bow down to You!

Aarti of Lakshmiji (optional)

ॐ जय लक्ष्मी माता मैया जय लक्ष्मी माता।
तुमको निसिदिन सेवत हर विष्णु-धाता ॥ ॐ ॥

om jaya lakshmee maataa maiyaa jaya lakshmee maataa
tum ko nisi din sevata har vishnu dhaataa

May Maa Lakshmee ever prevail! You are always served by Shankara, Vishnu, and Brahma.

उमा, रमा, ब्रह्माणि, तुम ही जग-माता।
सूर्य-चन्द्रमा ध्यावत, नारद ऋषि गाता ॥ ॐ ॥

umaa, ramaa, brahmaani, tum hee jaga maataa
soorya chandramaa dhyaavata, naarada rishi gaataa

You are Uma, Ramaa, and Brahmaani (divine consorts of Shankara, Vishnu and Brahma respectively) in Your varied forms. You are the Mother of the Universe. The Sun and the Moon meditate upon You (and thus derive their light and energy).

Sage Narada sings Your praises (and educates others about You)

दुर्गारूप निरंञ्जनि सुख-सम्पत्ति-दाता।
जो कोई तुमको ध्यावत, ऋधि -सिधि-धन पाता ॥ॐ॥

durgaa roopa niran jani sukha sammpati daataa
jo koi tumko dhyaavat, ridhi sidhi dhana paataa

In form of Goddess Durga, You are the bestower of happiness and wealth. Whoever meditates upon You is blessed with Enlightenment and Accomplishment (knowledge and success).

तुम पाताल -निवासिनि, तुम ही शुभदाता ।
कर्म-प्रभाव-प्रकाशिनि, भवनिधि की त्राता ॥ॐ॥

tum paataal nivaasini, tum hi subha daataa
karma prabhaav prakaa shini, bhava nidhi kee traataa

You dwell in the Nether- World (land of sorrow and darkness). Yet, You alone bestow auspiscious blessings. You illumine the effect of karma, (causing one's deeds to fruition). You grant salvation to the soul from the ocean of material existence, and the repetetive cycle of birth and death.

जिस घर तुम हो रहती, सब सद्‌गुण आता।
सब सम्भव हो जाता, मन नहिं घबराता ॥ॐ॥

jis ghar tum ho rahtee, saba sada guna aataa

saba sambhava ho jaataa, mana nahin ghaba raataa

All virtues arrive in the home You choose to kindly dwell. All accomplishments become possible, and the mind is purged of fear.

|| तुम बिन यज्ञ न होते, वस्त्र न हो पाता।
खान-पान का वैभव सब तुम से आता ॥ॐ॥ ||

tum bina yagya na hotey, vastra na ho paataa
khaan paan kaa vaibhav saba tum se aataa

No fire-sacrifice (yagya) can be performed without You. No clothing is possible without You. (No deed is worth doing without the reward of success and fruition, which is You, Maa! Clothing of protection from external environment, and projection of one's wealth and status too, is not possible without the Your grace of accomplishment). All forms of oppulence, and fulfilment of desires, both of the body (khaan, food) and of the mind (paan,liquid) are born out of You, Maa!

|| शुभ-गुण-मन्दिर सुन्दर, क्षीरोदधि -जाता
रत्न चतुर्दश तुम, बिन कोई नही पाता ॥ॐ॥ ||

shubha guna mandir sundar, ksheero dadhi jaataa
ratna chaturdasha tum bin koi nahin paataa

You reside in the beautiful Temple of Auspiscious Virtues, located in the Ocean of Milk (of virtuous living). None other than You grant the 14 jewels (of success and accomplishments in life).

महालक्ष्मी (जी) की आरती, जो कोई नर गाता।
उर आनन्द समाता, पाप उतर जाता ॥ॐ॥

mahaa lakshmeeji ki aartee, jo koi nar gaataa
ur aanand samaataa, paap utar jaataa

Whoever sings the praise of Maha Lakshmee and lives his life as Her blessing, is filled with joy in his heart, and is purged of all sins (shortcomings).

Keep the aarti plate down. Take a spoon of water. Make a circle over the plate with the water filled spoon. Pour the water in front of the pooja-plate on the ground. Say:

आआर्र्तिक्यम् समर्पयामि।

aar aarti kyam samar payaami

I offer aarti to You

ॐ गणेशाम्बिकादि सहितं सर्वेभ्यो आवाहित् प्रतिष्ठित्
देवताभ्यो नमः। ततः प्रधान् देवता महा लक्ष्मी देव्यै नमः॥

om ganesha ambikaa di sahitam
sarvey bhyo aavaa hit pratish thit devataa bhyo namah
tatah pradhaan devata mahaa lakshmee devyei namah

I bow to Lord Ganesha, Maa Paarvati, along with all the invoked deities and the presiding deity Maha Lakshmee.

You may cup your palms over the flame and then caress your forehead and face with your palm, as if to spread the warmth of blessings thus obtained. Other persons present may do the same.

Pushpaanjali (palm-full floral offerings)

All family and friends present at the poojaa should take petals of flowers in their hands and say:

|| ॐ एकदंताय विद्महे वक्रतुण्डाय
धीमहि तन्नो दंतीः प्रचोदयात्। ||

om eka dan taaye vid mahey
vakra tun daaye dhee mahi
tanno dantihi pracho dayaat

Ganesh Gayatri: I meditate on the One-Toothed Lord, whose trunk is bent. May He lead and guide me.

|| त्वमेव माता च पिता त्वमेव त्वमेव बन्धुश्च सखा त्वमेव।
त्वमेव विद्या द्रविणं त्वमेव त्वमेव सर्वं मम देव देव॥ ||

twameva maataa cha pitaa twameva
twameva bandhush cha sakhaa twameva
twameva vidya dravinam twameva
twameva sarvam mam deva deva

You alone are the Mother and the Father, Your are the Family and the best Friend. You alone are the Knowledge, You alone the Wealth, You alone are my All, Oh God! Oh Mother!

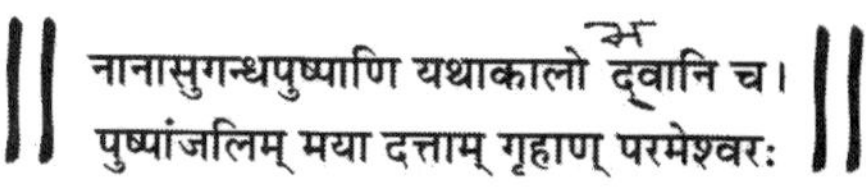
॥ नानासुगन्धपुष्पाणि यथाकालो द्भवानि च।
पुष्पांजलिम् मया दत्ताम् गृहाण् परमेश्वरः ॥

naanaa sugandhi push paani yathaa kaalod bhavaani cha
pushpaan jalim mayaa dattam grahaan parmesh warah

I offer flowers of various fragrances gathered in my palm to You, Maa Bhavaani! May You please accept my humble palm-full of floral offerings.

॥ ॐ गणेशाम्बिकादि सहितं सर्वेभ्यो आवाहित् प्रतिष्ठित्
देवताभ्यो नमः। ततः प्रधान् देवता महा लक्ष्मी देव्यै नमः॥ ॥

om ganesha ambikaa di sahitam
sarvey bhyo aavaa hit pratish thit devataa bhyo namah
tatah pradhaan devata mahaa lakshmee devyei namah

I bow to Lord Ganesha, Maa Paarvati, along with all the invoked deities and the presiding deity Maha Lakshmee.

Pradakshina (circumbulation)

Meditate on the wheel turning around the axis. Meditate on Goddess as the axis, and you wrapping around Her feet, or simply turning around Her as a wheel. Meditate on the Wheel of Life, the Wheel of Time, the Wheel of Good Fortune, turning around Mother Goddess. Stand up and turn from your left to your right in clockwise direction. Make 3 rotations. Say:

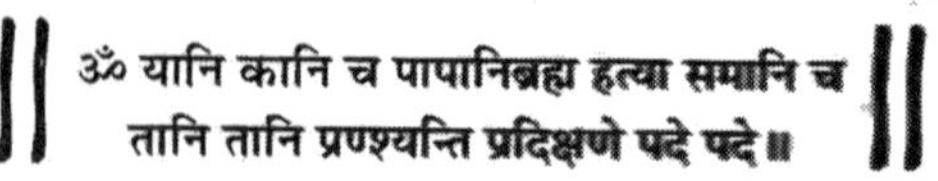

om yaani kaani cha paapani
brahma hatyaa samaani cha
taani taani pranayashanti
pradak shiney padey padey

Whatever sins I have committed, even the most grim and ghastly, may each be destroyed with each step of my circumbulation. May I be purified, and reshaped by Goddess, as fresh clay on potter's wheel is transformed into a beautiful piece of pottery, having lost all impurities it had as mud

Shaanti Paath (Prayers for Peace and Happiness of All Beings)

Meditate on a wave of peace spread over the entire world. All present may say;

तम्सो मा ज्योतिर्गमय
असतो मा सद्गमय
मृत्योर्मामृतम् गमय

tamso ma jyotir gamaya
asato ma sad gamaya
mrityur ma amritam gamaya

(Optional)

ॐ सहना ववतु सहनौ भुनक्तु सहवीर्यम् कर्वावहै
तेजस्विना वधीतमस्तु मा विदविषा वहै

om saha naa vavatu,
saha nau bhunaktu,
saha veer yam karavaa vahai
tejas vinaa vadheeta mastu
maa vidvishaa vahai

ॐ सर्वेषाम् स्वस्ति भवतु
सर्वेषाम् शान्तिर्भवतु
सर्वेषाम् पूर्णम् भवतु
सर्वेषाम् मंगलम् भवतु

om sarvey shaam svasti bhavatu
sarvey shaam shantir bhavatu
sarvey shaam poornam bhavatu
sarvey shaam mangalam bhavatu

ॐ पूर्णमदः पूर्णमिदं पूर्णात् पूर्ण मुदच्यते
पूर्णस्य पूर्णमादाय पूर्णमेव वाशिष्यते।

om poorna madah poorna midam
poornaat poorna muda chyatey
poornasya poorna maa daaya
poorna meva vashish yatey

om shantihi shantihi shantihi

From darkness (of ignorance), take us to light (of knowledge),

From untruth (of seeking fulfillment in the temporary world), take us to Truth (of self-realisation, and source of all fulfillment),

From death(of our bodies), take us to immortality (realisation of our immortal Self, the Soul)

May there be peace, may there be peace, may there be peace!

Kshama Prarthana (Offering apology and seeking forgiveness)

Meditate on the Mother Goddess and seek Her loving forgiveness for any fault in performing Her ritual worship. In fact, every deed of ours, every act is our offering to Her. Errors should be recognised, rectified and never repeated. That is true repentance. Maa's grace and forgiveness is reflected in our actions becoming closer to perfection. Fold your hands and say:

|| नमस्ते सर्वदेवानां वरदासि हरिप्रिये।
या गतिस्त्वत्प्रपन्नानां सा मे भूयात्वदर्चनात्॥ ||

namastey sarva devaa naam vardaasi hari priye

yaa gatis twat pra pannaa naam
sa mey bhooyaat tav dar chanaat

आवाह्नं न जानामि न जानामि विसर्जनम्।
पूजां चैव न जानामि क्षमस्व परमेश्वरि।

aavaa hanam na jaa naami na jaa naami visar janam
poojaam chaiva na jaa naami kshama sva param eshwari

मन्त्रहीनं क्रियाहीनं भक्तिहीनं सुरेश्वरि।
यत्पूजितं मया देवि परिपूर्णं तदस्तु मे॥

mantra heenam kriyaa heenam bhakti heenam suresh wari
yat poojitam mayaa devi pari poornam tadastu mey

अज्ञानाद्विस्मृतेर्भ्रान्त्या यन्न्यूनमधिकं कृतम्।
तत्सर्वं क्षम्यतां देवि प्रसीद परमेश्वरि॥

agyaanaa dwi smriteyer bhraan tyaa yan
nyoonam adhikam kritam
tat sarvam kshamya taam devi praseeda param eshwari

कामेश्वरि जगन्मातः सच्चिदानन्दविग्रहे।
गृहाणार्चामिमां प्रीत्या प्रसीद परमेश्वरि॥

kaamesh wari jagan maatah sacchi daa nanda vigrahey
grihaa naar chaa mimaam preetyaa praseeda parame shwari

गुह्यातिगुह्यागोप्त्री त्वं गृहाणास्मत्कृतं जपम्।
सिद्धिर्भवतु मे देवि त्वत्प्रसादात्सुरेश्वरि॥

guhyaati guhya goptri twam grihaana smat kritam japam
siddhir bhavatu mey devi twat prasaadaat suresh wari

I know not how to invite You, Maa, nor how to bid You farewell Nor do I know how to offer You my prayers, please forgive Oh Goddess!!

My worship has been with impure mantras, rituals, and devotion. Please make them complete and pure, and accept them yet as mine!!

Dedication

We offer the dedication of our worship to Bhagwaan Vishnu. Meditate on Vishnu and say:

|| कायेनवाचा मनसेन्द्रियेर्वा
बुद्धात् मनवप्रकृतेः स्वभावात्
करोमि यद् यत् सकलम् परस्मै
नारायणायेति समर्पयामि। ||

Kayen vaacha manas endri yair va
Buddh yatmana va prakriteh sva bhaavaat
Karomi yadyat sakalam parasmai
Naaraa yanaa yeti samar payaami

Whatsoever I perform with my body, words, mind or senses Or intellect or nature, I dedicate to

Bhagwaan Naaraayana

Visarjan (Conclusion of the Pooja)

Meditate on all the deities being thanked and bid farewell to. Place your hand gently over the yantra and the supari in the pooja-plate. Say:

om anen yathaa shaktya archa nen
shree maha lakshmeehi prasee datu

येन बद्धो बली राजा दानवेन्द्रो महाबलः।
ते नत्वामनुबध्नामि रक्षे माचल माचल ॥

yaantu deva ganaaha sarvey poojaa maadaaya maam keem
ishta kaama samridhya artham punaraa gama naaya cha

gachcha gachcha sur sreshthey swa sthanam parmey shwari
poojaa raadhan kaaley cha punaraa gama naaya cha

Gently shake the supari and the yantra and also the kalasha, as if all deities are leaving. Take a spoon of water and put under your worship seat, touch the floor with the tip of your fingers and touch your forehead thereafter.

Oh Foremost amongst Deities! May You depart and reach Your abode, Goddess!

Whenever I invoke You for worship, please do come again and bless me with Your presence.

Raksha Sootra Bandhanam (Tie mauli)

Ask someone to tie mauli (red thread, also called kalava). Mauli has to be tied on your right wrist. Take a pinch of rice and flowers in your right hand and clench your fist closed. Keep the palm side facing downwards, while mauli is being tied. Then, put the rice and petals in the pooja-plate. Thereafter, you may tie mauli to all present in a similar manner. You may also put tilak on everyone's forehead.

While tying mauli, meditate on divine protection and say:

येन बद्धो बली राजा दानवेन्द्रो महाबलः ।
ते नत्वामनुबध्नामि रक्षे माचल माचल ॥

yen baddho bali raaja daanav endro mahaa balah
tey natwa manu bagh naami rakshey maachala maachala

The protective thread that was tied on the most mighty King Bali, I tie on you too, so that you are ever protected.

Prasada (The Blessings)

Now, distribute sweets and fruits as prasada (the pleasure and blessings of Goddess) to all present. Give with your right hand, into their right hands. Joyfully eat and celebrate!

Daana (Offerings to Charity)

It would be beneficial if you take out some money and send to charity of your choice.

There is a universal law- you reap what you sow, you get what you give. If you need a tree, you need to plant only a tiny seed. If you need a harvest of crops, you need to sow a few seeds, plant a few saplings. If you need love, you have to give love. If you need respect, you have to give respect. Similarly, if you need wealth, you have to give away wealth selflessly to charity. Deepaawali being a festival of Goddess of Wealth, Maa Mahaa Lakshmee, you have prayed for Her to bless you with wealth.

Offerings India supports Sadhuwan Foundation. Your donations will be gratefully accepted. It will be used towards building the temple of Goddess Mahaa Lakshmee Shri Vidya, along with the Centre of Silence for meditation and spiritual education. It is located at Voda Mahadev temple, Noida, India. Sadhuwan Foundation has other social initiatives like health education in the villages around the temple, and primary medical care. There is a gurukul that imparts vedic education to young children from the village.

If you so wish, you may send your donation to
Sadhuwan Foundation,
A-81, Sector-26, NOIDA-201 301 (UP)
India

Office/ Shop/ Factory Pooja (optional)

Mantra Japa, and Meditation (optional)

The night of Deepaawali is considered very auspicious for performing deeper spiritual practices, as learnt from qualified Masters (Gurus). Those of you who chant specific mantras or do special practices, may wish to take out sometime around mid night to sit in meditation and perform those practices. For those of you who do not have any specific mantra to chant, yet may want to practice on Deepaawali night, the following simple mantra and practice may be performed.

1. Sit comfortably, with your back firm and straight. You may sit cross-legged on a soft seat put on the floor, or may sit on the edge of a chair, with your spine straight. Keep your hands in your lap, or on your knees, palm-side up. Keep your eyes gently closed.

2. Relax your forehead, your face, your shoulders, your back and full body.

3. Breathe evenly, with your stomach rising and falling.

4. Draw your attention to your breath. ONLY OBSERVE your breath. DO NOT CONTROL your breath. Observe as the breath enters your nostrils, touches the skin, travels deep in. Observe as the breath leaves the nostril, to return again.

5. Stabilise your breath. Breathe gently. Do not use force. Do not break your breath, either when you breathe in or when you breathe out.

6. When your mind is calm and reasonably composed, gently begin to chant any one of the fol-

lowing mantras for as long as you wish, without counting:

ॐ नमः शिवाय।

om namah shivaaya

|| हरे राम हरे राम राम राम हरे हरे
हरे कृष्ण हरे कृष्ण कृष्ण कृष्ण हरे हरे ||

hare raama hare raama raama raama hare hare
hare krishna hare krishna krishna krishna hare hare

ॐ ऐं ह्रीं क्लीं चामुण्डायै विच्चे।

om ain(g) hreen(g) kleen(g) chaamun daayee vichhey

Gratitude

I offer my deepest gratitude at the lotus feet of my Gurudeva, Mahamandaleshwara Swami (Dr)Veda Bharati, D.Litt (Holland), Disciple of Swami Rama of the Himalayas, for His grace and blessings. I am grateful to Dr Brajesh Tiwary who helped me with selecting the mantras for this work, and translation of some portions, which surpassed my humble understanding. I am grateful to all the vedic scholars and sages who have long passed into the realm of ancient immortality, for having left behind such indelible footprints in the sands of time, which are valid even today, as a path to Higher Life and God. Above all, my prayers to Maa Maha Lakshmee, to accept this work as my offerings of petals of devotion. May She bless all.